CREATING A HOME

PAINT FINISHES
FOR HOME DECORATORS

WARD LOCK

CONTENTS

5 Introduction
7 Ragging and rag rolling
11 Sponging
15 Colourwashing
19 Spattering
23 Dragging
27 Stippling
31 Crackleglaze effects
35 Watercolour washes
39 Combing
43 Using wood stains
47 Scumbling
49 Dry scumbling
53 Marbling
57 Bambooing
61 Tortoiseshelling
65 Porphyry
67 The art of stencilling
71 Stencilling borders
77 Spray stencilling
83 Block printing
87 Painting on furniture
91 Painting frames
95 Index/Photographic credits

© Ward Lock Limited, 1993
A Cassell Imprint
Villiers House, 41-47 Strand, London WC2N 5JE
Reprinted 1994
Based on *Creating A Home*
First Edition © Eaglemoss Publications Limited, 1986

ISBN 0 7063 7205 0

Printed in Spain by Cayfosa Industria Grafica

INTRODUCTION

The current popularity of those special-effect paint finishes which were once the province of the professional decorator has encouraged more and more people to try their hand at these traditional techniques.

Paint finishes for home decorators proves that even the amateur can master the skills needed to create a wonderful variety of effects on walls and doors, floors and furniture. An exciting alternative to plain paint or wallpaper, many of these finishes are extremely practical, too, providing a handy disguise for uneven walls, giving a new look to a tired decorating scheme, and adding a touch of class to flat-pack furniture.

From straightforward sponging through to more ambitious totoiseshelling, each technique is fully explained. Colour photographs illustrate each step and small-scale projects suggest ways of trying out your new-found skills. If mixing colours is not your strong point, there are plenty of design hints to help you make your choice.

For the absolute beginner, the early chapters cover some of the simplest and quickest paint finishes: sponging, ragging, colourwashing and, most fun of all, spatter painting! Their random appearance makes them the ideal choice for a first attempt since small irregularities tend not to show.

Dragging, stippling and combing are just some more of the more adventurous finishes you will be inspired to try. In addition, there are 'fantasy effects' – surprising look-alike techniques that can give a wooden floor the feel of marble, a dull picture frame the luxury of tortoiseshell!

Ever popular and infinitely versatile, the art of stencilling gets the coverage it deserves, with three chapters and full-size patterns for you to trace to make your own stencils.

Not for the faint-hearted, the final chapters show how you can have fun with freehand painting, transforming old furniture and shabby household objects into original works of art!

Ragging and rag rolling

A scrunched up rag rolled in parallel lines or dabbed over a wet paint surface creates a decorative design on walls, ceilings and furniture that echoes moiré or crushed velvet. Ragging gives a haphazard pattern, while rag rolling is used for a more regular effect.

Ragging and rag rolling are simple and quick to do and require little equipment. The subtle patterns can look more interesting than plain walls without imposing on the decor of a room as some wallpaper designs do. Both techniques are ideal for disguising uneven or blemished walls. They can also be used on furniture; but rag rolling should only be done where the repeat pattern will show up.

A variety of effects

Effects can be delicate or dramatic. For example, using two colours at the same time gives a subtle effect, while leaving one coat to dry before applying the next creates a more striking contrast.

▽ *The subtle effects created by ragging add warmth and texture to the walls of a dressing room.*

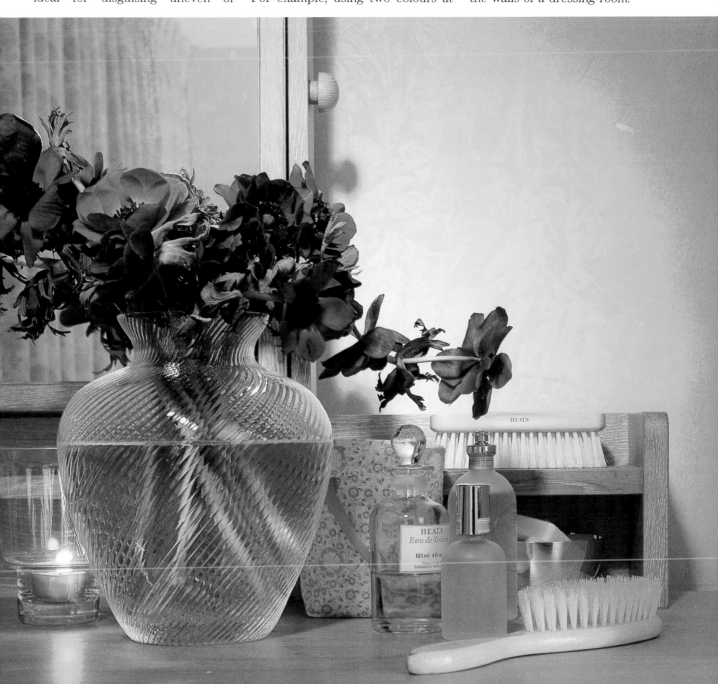

Preparation

Rags become clogged and need replacing as you work so have a number ready cut. An ideal size is about 8in (20cm) x 12in (30cm). Use rags of the same material to complete the job as a change in fabric will show up in the design. When you are cutting up the rags, remove all hems, seams and stitched areas, as these will spoil the finished paint effect.

The rag material and the colours you use both decide the strength or subtlety of the pattern. To make sure that you will be happy with the result, it is a good idea to do some samples on lining paper first. Tape these in position on the surface to be decorated and check the effect in both day and night light before making a decision on which scheme to use.

△ *Rolling is most effective over large areas as it produces a consistent repeat pattern. This makes it perfect for use on walls and ceilings.*

△ *Ragging forms a haphazard design which creates an all-over effect. It is ideal for use on small areas such as skirting boards, chairs and tables.*

A successful finish

While ragging, it is best to change the position of your hand to avoid the creases in the rag creating a design that is too repetitive.

When rag rolling, make sure that you fold the rag so that there are enough creases to create the right effect. It is best to turn in the rag ends and loosely crumple it in your hands. The rag will form a sausage shape when rolled up the wall.

Rag rolling gives a regular repeat pattern but the rag-rolled lines do not need to be straight; a slightly wavy line often gives the best effect. The lines must be vertical — if they go off at a tangent they will be very noticeable.

On a large area such as a wall, establish your first rag-rolled line by using a plumb line and bob. This gives you a straight edge to follow, and is the best guide as you cannot mark the wet wall. You will only

◁ *Ragging is the perfect technique for decorating country homes. The random swirls create a rustic atmosphere which complements the wooden fireplace and floral chairs.*

Method

Firstly, the surface is painted with an eggshell base coat and allowed to dry thoroughly. A glaze is made up by mixing a second colour, or a deeper or lighter tone of the first, with an oil glaze. This is then painted over the base coat. While this is still wet, a clean, scrunched-up rag is used to make the design.

Ragging involves dabbing the wet glaze with the rag, while rag rolling requires the rag to be rolled up the wall in vertical lines, each just overlapping the pre-vious one. The rag removes some of the wet glaze from the surface and, depending on which technique you have used, reveals the base colour beneath in either a regular or random design.

The paint must be worked on before it starts to be-come tacky. You can do ragging or rag rolling on your own, although rag rolling especially is best done by two people. The oil glaze is applied by one person working down the wall in a strip, while the second fol-lows behind forming the design with the rag.

△ *A crumpled rag is rolled up the wall in one movement, forming a stripe. The process is repeated, overlapping the pattern slightly each time.*

△ *A rag is loosely scrunched up and patted over the prepared wall, removing the glaze in patches. This reveals the colour beneath, creating a mottled print.*

need to do this once as repeat lines are not difficult to keep vertical; they will simply follow the direction of the first one.

If a ragged area is splashed while applying the ground coat of oil glaze to a nearby area, just dab the mark so that it blends in. If the glaze on any of the ragged areas is too thin, brush paint over this area and rag once more.

Colour combinations

When planning your colour scheme, bear in mind that the best results are created by using a lighter shade as the base colour and ragging or rag rolling a darker shade over the top. Create extra interest by re-versing the colours in some areas; for example, use light colours over dark on mantelpieces and shelves.

The safest way to achieve a suc-cessful result is to combine two tones of the same colour; for ex-ample, try ragging terra cotta over burnt umber for a warm look, or use a deep sky blue over a pale blue for a cooler effect. By ex-perimenting with colour com-binations you can create different moods and effects: lemon yellow over citrus green will produce a vibrant scheme, whereas cream on golden yellow will be subtle

Try ragging pale grey or blue over white for a pastel scheme, or aqua on light green for a tranquil effect. Alternatively, rag apricot over cream for a more cosy feel. To create dramatic contrasts, try navy or wine on a white background, or use pale blue over poppy red.

Materials

Rags

Unglazed cotton is the traditional material for producing this finish, and old cotton sheets are ideal. To rag roll an average size room 12ft sq (3.65m sq), you need one torn up single sheet. A fabric made up totally from man-made fibres is not suitable as it will not absorb the paint. However, fabric that contains a small proportion of synthetic fibres, such as a cotton polyester, works well. Experiment with dif-ferent materials; for example, J cloths, chamois and linen.

Transparent oil glaze

Also known as scumble glaze, transparent oil glaze slows down the drying process of the paint. It also helps to give the top coat a transparency impossible to repro-duce in any other way. It can only be mixed with oil-based paints (those that can only be removed from brushes by using white spirit).

◢ TIP	SAFETY

Ragging or rag rolling a room will leave you with a lot of paint-clogged rags. Ensure that these are dry before throwing them away as rags still soaked in wet paint are a fire hazard. After using white spirit, ensure that its lid is firmly screwed on, and that it is kept in a safe place out of children's reach.

A striped bathroom

The beautiful and unusual appearance of this bathroom is created by rag rolling subtle grey stripes over a magnolia base.

You will need

◇ 4in (10cm) paint brush
◇ Eggshell paint in base colour
◇ Eggshell paint in top colour
◇ Transparent oil glaze
◇ White spirit
◇ Paint kettle for mixing glaze
◇ Rags cut into squares
◇ Plastic sheets or newspapers
◇ Rags for mopping up
◇ Rubber gloves
◇ Plumb line and bob

1 Prepare the surface by filling any cracks and holes with filler. Brush on the base coat and leave to dry. If there is a contrast to the colour underneath, you may need to apply two coats. Allow to dry well.

2 Using a plumb line and bob, mark straight lines down the wall a distance of about 8in (20cm) apart. Protect the areas that aren't going to be rag rolled by covering with masking tape.

△ *The subtle colours of this rag-rolled design add an air of freshness and height to a bathroom.*

3 Make up the glaze from 20% grey eggshell, 70% oil glaze and 10% white spirit. Sand the base coat lightly to ensure a key for the paint and clean down with a rag dipped in white spirit.

4 One person should apply the top coat of paint using long, vertical brush strokes, while the other follows on, rag rolling from the bottom to the top of each stripe in one movement.

5 Stand back and check that the ragging design covers the stripes evenly. If there are any spaces in the pattern, fill in by lightly touching-up with the rag.

▽ *The rag-rolled stripes on the wall emphasize the vertical wooden panels. The panels themselves have been rag rolled in the same way for a co-ordinated finish.*

Sponging

Walls, woodwork, furniture and accessories can all be transformed with this attractive paint effect. Partly covering the surface, it allows a toning or contrasting base colour to show through. This type of finish is also an excellent disguise for slightly uneven surfaces.

What is sponging?

This is a quick and easy technique in which one or more colours are applied with a slightly dampened sponge over a solid base colour. A natural sponge is best; a synthetic sponge can be used if you tear it to an irregular shape and apply the paint with the inner surface.

You can create subtle or striking results depending on the colours you choose, the spaces between the sponge marks and the size of the sponge. It is usual to sponge a darker colour over a lighter base but it is quite possible to work the other way around.

Contrasting colours give dramatic effects whereas closely related tones will create a more subtle textured finish. Sponging with just one colour can look rather 'spotty', unless the sponged colour is closely related to the base coat — apricot on warm yellow, for example, or rust on pale terracotta.

In general, two or more sponged colours give a more pleasing effect than one. Always try out various colourways before starting work on a project. It is advisable to have a few strips of lining paper or scrap paper on hand to experiment on; keep these efforts and a note of the colours for reference later.

Materials

Emulsion and oil-based paint
For beginners, it is a good idea to experiment first with emulsion paint only. Emulsion is a water-based paint and is much less trouble to prepare and to clean up. When you are confident, you can progress to using oil-based paints and scumble glaze.

Scumble glaze
Traditionally, broken paint effects have been created using a scumble glaze. This commercial product is a transparent glaze which is tinted with artists' oil-based paints or Universal stainers, then applied

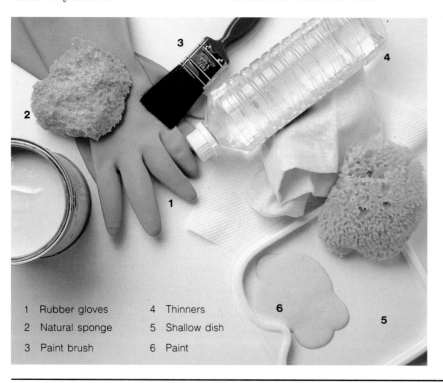

1	Rubber gloves	4	Thinners
2	Natural sponge	5	Shallow dish
3	Paint brush	6	Paint

Sponging a tray

A simple wooden tray makes a good starting project for sponging.

You will need
- ◇ 4in (100mm) paint brush
- ◇ **Emulsion** base coat/ sponging coat
- ◇ Thinner — water
- ◇ **Eggshell** base coat/ sponging coat
- ◇ Thinner — white spirit
- ◇ Scrap paper for testing
- ◇ Shallow dish
- ◇ Natural or synthetic sponge
- ◇ Plastic sheets/ newspapers
- ◇ Rags for mopping up
- ◇ Rubber gloves
- ◇ Polyurethane gloss (optional for sealing the finished tray when using emulsion)

4 Lightly dab the sponge over the surface. Turn the sponge as you work in order to vary the pattern. If you are sponging with just one colour you should keep the marks fairly close together. If you are using two or more colours you can space them out a little more.

5 Recharge the sponge with paint whenever necessary, testing it on a piece of scrap paper each time before recommencing your work. Re-start sponging in a corner or inconspicuous place in case the new sponge mark blurs. If you start in the middle of an area, it might be obvious if the first sponge marks were too heavy.

over an oil-based base coat (usually a matt paint such as eggshell). Since the glaze is semi-transparent, even when tinted, it allows the base colour to glow through, giving a rich warm finish to your walls, woodwork and furniture. This technique will be covered in detail on pages 48 and 54.

Sponging different surfaces

As a rule you should not mix different types of paint. Remember always to use oil-based on oil-based paints and water-based on water-based paints.

For sponging on walls, you can use emulsion paint. Applying the base coat is easy using a roller or pad. For the sponged coat, emulsion paint can be applied straight from the tin. However, you will achieve a softer colour effect if you dilute the paint with a little water.

On small items, woodwork, or in kitchens and bathrooms, which are subject to heavy condensation, eggshell paint is a good choice. As this is an oil-based paint, apply the base coat with a brush. Before sponging, thin the second eggshell colour with a little white spirit to make the coverage easier.

<table>
<tr><td>

TIP **PUTTING IT RIGHT**

◇ A less-than-perfect result can easily be improved. If you have sponged on too much colour, sponge on a little of the base coat.

◇ You can give a too-subtle effect more impact by adding a considerably darker shade or a lighter shade or even a contrast colour.

</td></tr>
</table>

1 Prepare the surface of the tray and paint on the base coat. Leave to dry thoroughly.

2 Pour a little sponging colour into a shallow dish. Dip the sponge into water and squeeze it thoroughly. Then dip it into the paint and squeeze to remove excess paint.

3 Experiment with the colour on scrap paper to discover the sort of effect you want — try the paint diluted or straight from the tin to see which provides the best results. Keep dabbing until the sponge leaves a soft speckled mark. The sponge should be almost dry so that the marks show; if it is too wet the paint will blur or run.

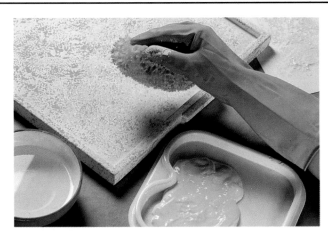

6 Apply a second sponged coat when the previous one is quite dry. Fill in gaps between prints and also overlap some to blend the colours.

▷ *The base colour for the tray is very pale apricot; the first sponged colour is Wedgwood blue and the second is soft peach.*

13

Harmonious colour combinations A Wedgwood blue base coat sponged with soft pink (*left*) and then lilac (*above*).

Contrasting colours A dove grey base coat sponged with darker grey (*above*) and then rich buttermilk

Similar colours — dark on light and light on dark A soft green base coat sponged with mid then dark green (*left*). The order is reversed (*above*).

Colourwashing

'Colourwash' is a broad term used to describe any decorating technique that involves painting one colour over another so that the base colour shows through. Before the days of pre-mixed household paints, diluted lime tinted with pigments was used for colourwashing.

The secret of successful colourwashing is confidence and bold brush strokes. With these two vital ingredients, even beginners can achieve stunning results. Once you have started painting a wall or other surface, keep going: never try to touch up or go back over what you have already done as small irregularities will not show once the work is finished.

The best colourwashes are produced by painting a transparent glaze over a base colour and then partially removing it to reveal the colour beneath. Diluted emulsions and other household paints can be used instead of glaze, but they are more difficult to apply and less effective because they lack the translucent glow of real glazes.

The technique of colour washing is best suited to large areas such as walls, doors or big items of furniture. This is because the glaze is usually partially removed with a dry brush, using large random strokes. These sweeping strokes on a small surface are less effective and can be difficult to achieve. A cloth can also be used to remove the glaze, but this method is restricted to large areas of wall or ceiling in a room.

▷ *Be adventurous in your choice of colours for colourwashing. It is possible to use much bolder colours than you would normally choose, as a rich glaze will be softened by a paler base.*

Materials and equipment

Base colour

When choosing colours, the base coat is as important as the top coat of coloured oil glaze because it shows through the loose brush strokes and transparent glaze, affecting the final colour. A white base gives a light, airy look to the finished wall. A deep base colour creates a darker, intimate effect.

Glaze

Use an emulsion glaze over an acrylic or emulsion base coat, and an oil glaze over an eggshell base. For colourwashing, the glaze should be heavily diluted to a very thin, watery consistency. For further detail on emulsion glazes and information on the proportions used for making transparent glazes, see pages 9 and 24.

Brushes

An ordinary decorating brush can be used for applying the base and the glaze and for removing excess glaze. Alternatively, to produce a more textured effect, a specialist brush, such as a flogger or overgrainer, with widely spaced, tufted bristles, can be used to remove the glaze. A dry cloth gives a similar effect; see page 25.

Colourwashing

The following demonstrations used an eggshell base and an oil-based glaze. The glaze was made by mixing equal proportions of oil glaze and white spirit. Artists' oil paints were used to colour the glaze.

Basic colourwash technique

1 Using a decorating brush, apply the glaze solution to the base colour with loose brush strokes.

2 While the glaze is still wet, take a dry brush and go over the surface with quick random strokes to remove some of the paint and to soften the effect.

Two colour effect

When two colours are used they combine to make a third colour. By 'mixing' colours on the wall you can achieve beautiful effects of broken colour with flecks of the base colour showing through, instead of the flat, opaque look of pre-mixed colours.

1 Here, a bright yellow oil glaze is brushed over a strong magenta eggshell base. The result is a vivid glowing orange colour with flecks of yellow and magenta showing through in places.

2 Soften the glaze colour by working over the surface with a dry brush in the usual way.

Pattern and texture

You can create surface patterns by controlling the direction of the brush strokes. Wavy lines, criss-cross strokes and diagonal trellis patterns, for example, add interest to a large expanse of plain wall.

1 Apply the coloured oil glaze to the eggshell base coat in the normal way.

2 While the glaze is wet and workable, use the dry brush in various directional strokes to create the pattern of your choice.

A softening effect

For a more delicate, finer texture, slap the surface of the glaze, while it is still slightly wet, with the flat side of the brush. The technique is slower but gives a softer textured effect than basic colourwashing. This method is most suitable for smaller areas, such as doors or pieces of furniture.

1 Apply the base coat; allow to dry completely. Then paint on the coloured glaze.

2 Using a dry flogging brush or decorating brush, slap the flat side of the bristles sharply on to the wet glaze to break up the brush strokes and remove excess colour. Repeat this technique until you have covered the required area.

A striped effect

Although not a true colourwash, these stripes make a cheerful wall decoration using the same materials and techniques (see the previous pages).

1 Using two or more glaze colours, paint the stripes on to the base colour of the wall.

2 Drag a dry brush across the glazed surface in the same direction as the stripes to soften the edges.

DESIGN IDEAS

△ *A rich creamy yellow base, topped with a soft gold glaze, gives a warm glow.*

◁ *An aqua glaze over an off-white base forms a lively backdrop for this unusual panelled bath.*

18

Spattering

*Spattered paint is effective, easy and fun to do.
Whether you are painting a tiny object to give it a fine, multi-
coloured texture, or decorating a large piece of
furniture or a wall, spattering gives a lively, cheerful finish
that can brighten and enhance any type of surface.*

Spattering is very straightforward to do and the effect can be achieved with the most basic of materials. Most of us have spattered paint by accident and hastily mopped up the result. But deliberate spattering — building up droplets of paint to produce a textured surface pattern — is very creative and can produce beautiful, decorative results. An old brush or toothbrush and some paint are all you need to produce this versatile paint finish.

Materials and equipment
Paints

Almost any type of paint can be used for spattering, depending on the surface you are decorating. Whichever paint you choose, it should be mixed to the consistency of thick cream. Test the mixed paint before using it. If it is too thick the paint will tend to stick to the brush; if it is too thin it will form rivulets of colour and spoil the spattered effect.

Artists' oil paint is ideal for spattering and should be diluted to the right consistency with white spirit or turpentine. Oil paints can be used on top of emulsion or an oil-based paint, such as gloss. They are slow-drying and the paint should be allowed to dry before removing any masks to avoid smudging the spattered texture.

Acrylic paint When working with these quick-drying paints, mix only as much paint as you can use in one session as left-over paint dries hard and is wasted. Acrylics need to be diluted with water. They should not be used on top of an oil-based paint because the oily surface will eventually repel the acrylic paint and so spoil the finish.

Emulsion For painting and spattering large areas, household emulsion is economical and comes in a wide range of colours. But, like acrylics, it should not be spattered on top of an oil-based paint as the emulsion will be repelled by the oily surface.

Craft paints Enamels, fabric paints and cold ceramic colours should be diluted with the appropriate solvent. Follow the manufacturers' instructions regarding suitable surfaces.

Brushes

Spattering is usually done with a toothbrush or a decorating brush, depending on the size of the area to be painted. For wide expanses use a decorating brush or a large artists' brush. For small objects and fabric painting an old toothbrush is ideal because it allows more control over the final texture.

Surfaces

Suitable surfaces for spattering include fabric, walls, plastic, metal, wood, paper and porcelain. Obviously, the nature of the surface dictates the type of paint you choose, but all surfaces must be clean and well prepared before being decorated.

Spattered colours look best when applied over a flat colour. So an emulsioned wall, a plain fabric item or a piece of painted furniture are all ideal for decorating using the spattered paint technique.

Masks and stencils

Masking tape, paper masks and stencils can all be used to protect areas which are not to be painted. For straight lines and geometric shapes, masking tape is the most effective method, but you can also use cut-out stencils and torn paper as well as a variety of other flat shapes. For example, leaves, feathers and paper doilies have all been successfully used as alternative stencils for spatter painting.

Mixing colour

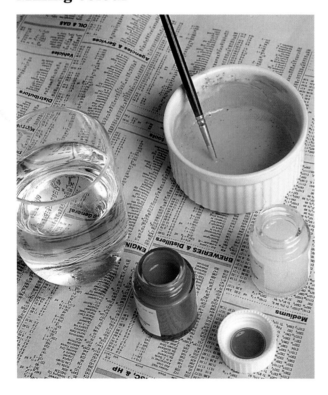

Mix enough colour for the job you are doing before starting to spatter. It is almost impossible to get exactly the same shade if you do run out of colour, so be sure to mix plenty at the outset. Use clean vessels, brushes and mixing sticks and store the paint in screw-topped jars for future use.

Toothbrush spattering

1 Place strips of masking tape on work surface to form desired shape; protect surrounding area with paper. Then load the toothbrush with paint: either paint it on to the toothbrush with a paint brush or dip the bristle tips in a shallow container of paint. Hold the loaded toothbrush a few inches from the surface and draw your thumb firmly backwards across the bristles to relase the paint.

2 Apply the second and any subsequent colours in the same way. If you are using the same toothbrush for each colour, make sure it is well washed and dried between each colour — working with a wet toothbrush causes the spattered paint to run.

3 When the paint is dry, carefully lift the masking tape at one corner and pull it upwards away from the painted surface.

Paint brush spattering

1 Use the jagged edge of a torn sheet of paper as a mask to produce an irregular shape. To create a coarsely textured effect, apply the spattered paint with a decorating brush. Dip the tips of the bristles into the paint. Then, holding the brush handle firmly in one hand, sharply tap the side of the brush against the side of your other hand to disperse the paint in large spatters over the surface.

2 Further colours can be added in the same way. To achieve a dense, heavy effect, hold the brush close to the surface; alternatively, for a lighter, sparser texture, lift the brush several inches clear of the painted surface.

3 When the paint is dry, carefully remove the mask from the spattered surface.

◇ TIP USING MASKS

◇ For geometric shapes, use masking tape to block areas not to be spattered. Press down the edges to prevent paint seeping underneath.

◇ Spattered paint covers a wide area, so protect the surrounds of the masked shape with sheets of paper or newspaper, taping them in place if necessary.

Using stencils

1 Choose a simple design and trace it on to a sheet of stiff paper, stencil film or card. Protect work surface with a cutting mat or heavy card and cut out the shapes with a sharp scalpel or craft knife.

2 Lay the stencil on the surface to be decorated and protect the surrounding area with sheets of paper. Spatter the colour over the cut-out design.

3 Leave the paint to dry completely, then carefully remove the stencil.

Mugs and tablecloth

Make teatime a colourful occasion with these co-ordinated mugs and tablecloth. Nothing could be simpler than this geometric pattern which borders the cloth and the white mugs. You could also decorate napkins and other items of tableware using the same motif.

You will need
◇ White mugs
◇ Plain white tablecloth
◇ Masking tape
◇ Fabric paints (pink, yellow and blue) and solvent
◇ Ceramic paints (pink, yellow and blue) and solvent
◇ Old toothbrush

Spattered mugs

1 Mask off the design by running two parallel strips of masking tape along the top of each mug, approximately ½in (1.2cm) apart. Join these at regular intervals with short diagonal strips of tape. Protect the rest of the mug with paper or masking tape.

2 Mix each ceramic paint colour to a creamy consistency, using the appropriate solvent. Use a toothbrush to spatter the paint.

3 When the paint is dry, remove the masking tape to reveal the multi-coloured spattered border.

Spattered tablecloth

Lay the tablecloth on a flat surface and decorate in the same way, using the fabric paints. Use masking tape for the design and protect plain areas of cloth with paper before starting work.

Dragging

The technique of dragging dates back to the 18th century, when it was used for wood-graining to produce a grain effect without actually exposing the bare wood. It is popular today as a decorative finish on doors, panels, walls, floors and larger pieces of furniture.

This traditional decorating technique is achieved by first applying a transparent or semi-transparent colour over a different base colour. Then, while the paint is still wet, a large, dry brush is 'dragged' across the surface with firm straight strokes so that the underneath colour shows through.

Dragging gives an unusual and creative finish.

△ *These kitchen cupboards have been painted using the technique of dragging. They contrast well with the walls, which have been painted to achieve a marbled effect.*

Materials and equipment

Paints

Paints with two different finishes are used in dragging: the opaque base coat and the transparent glaze which gives the grained finish. When choosing paint for dragging it is important to remember that there are two quite different types of paint — oil-based paints and water-based paints. The two types have different drying times and should never be mixed as they are totally incompatible. An oil-based paint must have an oil glaze, while a water-based paint needs to be followed by a water-soluble glaze.

Base colour

If you intend to finish with an oil glaze, use an eggshell paint for the base coat. If you cannot buy exactly the colour you want, it can be mixed to the correct shade using artists' oil paints. When using an emulsion glaze, the base coat should be an emulsion or acrylic paint.

Glaze

Oil glaze Available in tins, this is a thick, yellowish substance that resembles honey. Because the glaze has to be thin it should first be diluted with an equal quantity of white spirit or turpentine.

Oil glaze can discolour slightly with age. This is not usually severe enough to be a great disadvantage, but it is sometimes noticeable with pastel colours.

This transparent glaze mixture can be coloured with artists' oil paints or powder pigment to a strength to suit your chosen colour scheme. Mix in the colour thoroughly to prevent lumps of paint or powder pigment spoiling the finished effect. One problem with oil glaze is that it is extremely slow drying — the process can take several days if the painted surface is in an unheated room.

Emulsion glaze This is often used as a varnish to protect decorated finishes. When it is mixed with an equal amount of water, it can be used as a water-soluble glaze. Emulsion glaze looks white when wet but it becomes transparent when it dries. It can be coloured with watercolour, gouache, artists' acrylic or powder pigment. This glaze dries very quickly, making it unsuitable for use on large areas if you are working on your own. With two people, however, one person can apply the glaze while the other brushes the surface.

Brushes

The base colour can be applied with an ordinary decorator's paint brush — choose a size suitable for the area you are working on.

To produce the grained effect, a flogging brush, sometimes known as a dragging brush, is best. The bristles of these specialist brushes are very long and are arranged in tufts to give space between the lines of the dragged, paint effect.

Suitable surfaces

A dragged finish can be applied to most types of surface, although it is more difficult to get an even effect on small areas. Walls and household woodwork such as doors, skirting boards, floors and large items of furniture are all suitable subjects for dragging.

Preparing the surface

The surface to be painted should be well prepared, clean and free from loose particles. Wood should be rubbed down with sandpaper and new wood must be primed before applying the base colour.

Dragging

The following steps show the basic techniques of dragging and how to achieve the wood-grained effect. We used an eggshell base coat followed by an oil glaze. If you are using an emulsion or acrylic base coat with an emulsion glaze, follow the same basic steps.

2 Mix the glaze with equal parts of oil glaze and white spirit or turpentine. Add enough artists' oil paint to give you the colour you want. Mix the solution thoroughly and then apply it to the dry base colour.

3 While the glaze is still wet, take a dry flogging brush and drag this firmly across the glazed surface. Repeat this action, with the next strokes slightly overlapping the previous ones

1 Apply the base colour with a large decorating brush. The surface of the base coat of paint does not have to be absolutely flat, but care is needed to avoid uneven patches which can often show through the glaze. Leave to dry thoroughly.

4 Confidence is important when using the dragging technique, if you are to achieve straight, bold lines that reveal the base colour. Any hesitation will be reflected in the final pattern.

TIP SMALL ITEMS

If you are working on a small object or in a confined area, it may be easier to do the dragging using a rag instead of a flogging brush.

1 Apply the base colour as usual and leave to dry.

2 Scrunch up the rag and dip it in the transparent oil glaze mixture. Draw it over the surface in the same way as you would the brush.

Blanket box

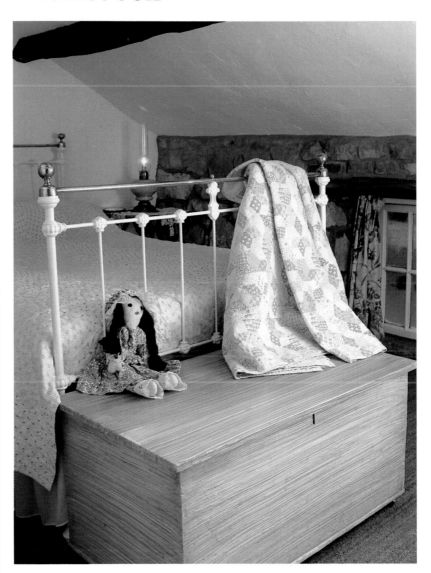

Add a touch of colour to an attic bedroom by dragging a plain wooden blanket box in the rich, russet hues of autumn colours.

You will need
◇ Wooden blanket box
◇ Pink eggshell paint
◇ Artists' oil paint
◇ Oil glaze
◇ White spirit
◇ Decorating brush
◇ Flogging brush
◇ Sandpaper
◇ Primer
◇ Varnish

1 Rub the blanket box down with sandpaper to roughen the surface and remove any loose particles of paint. The box pictured here is an old blanket chest. If you are painting a new box, with exposed wood, you will need to prepare it first with at least two coats of primer.

2 Paint the box with a coat of base colour. If this looks patchy, you may need a second coat. Leave to dry.

3 Make the transparent glaze mixture (see step 2 of the basic technique). Add artists' oil paint to achieve the colour of your choice.

4 Beginning with the larger, main surfaces first, paint the transparent glaze mixture over the base colour. While this is still wet, drag the surface using the dry flogging brush. When this is complete, drag the edges of the lid in the same way, using the narrow side of the brush.

5 Allow the glaze to dry completely. For a professional finish, protect the surface with two coats of varnish.

COLOUR LIBRARY

△ Create a warm, sunny look by dragging terracotta over an apricot base colour.

△ This tranquil effect has been created by painting a peppermint green colour over white.

△ Here, sky blue glaze has been dragged over a creamy-white base colour.

△ Alternatively, try dragging two colours, one over the other in opposite directions over the base coat.

Stippling

*Stippling involves dabbing a flat-faced brush
on to a wet, coloured glaze to lift speckles of glaze off
the surface and allow the base coat colour to
show subtly through. Furniture, walls and doors can all be
transformed with this delicate, flecked finish.*

The ever-popular technique of stippling combines two separate colours, one painted on top of the other, to give a soft paint effect. Despite the subtlety of the finished effect, this technique enables you to create a rich and exciting depth of colour that cannot be achieved with 'flat' coats of paint.

Materials and equipment
Stippling brushes
A specialist stippling brush is square in shape and has flat, fairly stiff bristles. It is rather costly, but creates a uniform effect. Stippling brushes come in a wide range of sizes — from those with a large surface area of bristles, to small, narrower ones. Choose a small brush for stippling furniture and a larger

A successful finish
Unlike sponging or ragging, which can conceal poor surfaces, stippling needs a smooth base; any unevenness will be highlighted. The paint glaze must be applied evenly, then the brush should be dabbed firmly on to the surface, working in vertical stripes. Do not try to cover too large an area at once; experiment on a small area first.

Stippling is easier if two people work together; one to apply the glaze and one to stipple it off. But make sure that there is no change in who brushes and who stipples, as any change is likely to show. Use a rag to clean the brush if it becomes saturated with glaze — but do not use white spirit part way through as this can cause the paint to run.

Stippling a filing cabinet
The smooth surface of a metal filing cabinet is ideal for stippling. This technique, worked in a colour to coordinate with its surroundings, will transform an ugly piece of furniture into a far more attractive item.

You will need
◇ 2in (5cm) paint brush
◇ Primer
◇ Eggshell paint in two colours
◇ Transparent oil glaze
◇ White spirit
◇ Rubber gloves
◇ Sandpaper
◇ Medium size stippling brush
◇ Plastic sheets or newspaper
◇ Rags for mopping up
◇ Polyurethane gloss varnish

3 Mix the top coat glaze using the correct proportions of the second eggshell colour, the transparent oil glaze and the white spirit.

4 Paint the glaze, applying it in vertical stripes over the side of the cabinet.

size for decorating walls.

Alternatively, experiment with any brush that has bristles of an even length, such as a shoe cleaning brush. A mohair or lambswool roller creates a similar, but softer and less defined look. On small areas, a flecked effect can also be achieved by using a synthetic sponge or a square of carpet.

Mixing the glaze
Use a mixture made up of 70 per cent transparent oil glaze (also known as scumble glaze), 10 per cent white spirit and 20 per cent eggshell paint (in the colour of your choice) for the top coat.

Alternatively, you can replace the eggshell with artists' oil colour. In this case, mix two parts of oil glaze to one part of white spirit.

First of all, mix the artists' oil colour separately with a little white spirit (add a small amount of white undercoat if you want to lighten the tone, or to stop it yellowing when added to the glaze). When you are satisfied with the colour, it can then be added to the glaze and stirred until well mixed.

Before mixing coloured glaze for a large area, test a small amount on a sheet of white paper.

Colour choice

Strong colours are a good choice for stippling, with one rich colour being used over another; a wine red stippled over bright pink creates a beautiful, warm look. Or try working royal blue over turquoise, for a more sophisticated effect.

Working a deep colour over white also looks effective: for example, stipple emerald green or bright yellow on white for a bright, fresh appearance. Do not use two pale or closely related colours over each other, as the effect of the stipple will be lost.

If the base is a light colour, stippling a deep glaze over the top will have the effect of softening and at the same time strengthening the base coat. For example, the overall effect of stippling a deep blue over white is mid-blue on pale blue. Alternatively, a room decorated in too strong a colour can be toned down by stippling a paler shade over the top. This effect was very popular during the 1930s.

1 Sand the surface and paint with a coat of primer suitable for metal. Leave to dry. Then lightly sand the surface to give a key for the paint.

2 Brush on the eggshell paint as a base coat. Allow the paint to dry thoroughly, sand again, and brush on a second coat. Leave to dry.

5 Starting from the base, and working upwards, stipple one side of the cabinet with a firm, jabbing movement. If you cause a streak, re-coat the mark with glaze and stipple over it.

6 After one side is finished, stipple the surface opposite to it in the same way. (This will help to prevent smudging the first side.) Continue in this way until all the surfaces are stippled.

7 Allow the paint to dry out completely for two days and then coat the stippled surface with clear, polyurethane varnish.

COLOUR LIBRARY

△ *Emerald green stippled over a white base colour.*

△ *Royal blue stippled over white.*

△ *Deep wine stippled over a sharp pink colour.*

△ *Terracotta stippled over gold.*

△ *White stippled over emerald green.*

△ *Cream stippled over terracotta.*

Crackleglaze effects

*When one type of paint or varnish is mixed
with another type, the two surfaces work against each
other to produce a pattern of hairline cracks
on the surface. This technique can be used to mimic age or
simply for its decorative appeal.*

It is now fashionable to reproduce the lovely, subtly crazed surfaces found on old pieces of furniture, oil paintings, or even walls and doors. Layers of paint or varnish can be used to create this effect. With the varnish method a water-based varnish is applied over an oil varnish, causing the surface to crack. The cracks can be highlighted by rubbing oil paint into the surface. Crackle varnish can be used on a plain painted surface or on a patterned surface, which will be visible beneath the varnish.

The crackle paint effect works on a similar principle, with the top layer cracking to reveal the layer beneath. Use subtle colours to age furniture or bold colours to produce purely fun effects. Both the crackle varnish and crackle paint techniques are covered here.

Traditional causes

The crazed surface on old painted furniture or oil paintings was formed either by the varying drying times of the materials used or by changing atmospheric conditions.

Oil paintings are a good example of the effect of varying drying times. The paint takes much longer than the protective varnish to dry, causing the varnish to crack.

In time, changes in temperature and humidity also cause painted surfaces to crack. Dust then lodges in the cracks, highlighting them and increasing the effect of age.

Crackle paint effect

This broken colour technique can be used to blend newly painted items with favourite, older, worn pieces of furniture. Alternatively, use it as a fun, decorative effect.

A base coat of one colour emulsion is painted on the surface and then covered with a layer of transparent gum arabic. Gum arabic is the magic ingredient that persuades the top coat to split open. When this has dried, a second colour emulsion is brushed over it.

Speed is essential as the water in the paint soon softens the dry gum arabic. To work, the layers must stay separated. The top layer starts to crack immediately to reveal the base colour in streaks and speckles.

What to decorate

Any item which can be painted is suitable, but you must experiment with colours and technique before you start. Use the finish to decorate door or cupboard frames, lamp bases, candle sticks and enamelware jugs. Do not use it to paint containers that are used for food, as water-based paint will not stand up to regular washing.

Colour choice

This finish looks most effective when contrasting colours are applied, or when it is used to show off different tones of one colour. Bear in mind that the streaks and splatters of the background colour may be lost if they are too subtle.

Materials and equipment

Emulsion paint Ordinary household emulsion paints (those thinned with water) can be used.

Gum arabic Most art shops sell water-colour gum arabic. You can also buy crystals which need to be dissolved in boiling water and then left to stand overnight to thicken slightly. Crackle paint kits, which include gum arabic, are available from large art and craft shops.

Protective finish As both methods end with a water-based layer, some protection is needed. The first part of the two-part crackle kit can be used as a final protective coating. Or use polyurethane varnish in matt or satin finish. Buff up with beeswax polish.

Crackle paint method

You will need

◇ Emulsion paint in two colours
◇ Paint brushes, about ½in (1.2cm) wide
◇ Water-colour gum arabic
◇ Washing-up liquid

1 Prepare the surface of the item to be painted so that it is clean, dry and completely free from grease. Apply a coat of the first colour emulsion and leave to dry thoroughly.

△ *The smaller items have all been painted using the crackle technique, while the door behind, cracked with age, was highlighted with a new wash of paint.*

▽ *Some of the crackle paint effects possible.*

2 Add a small drop of washing-up liquid to the gum arabic to stop it breaking open when applied; mix thoroughly. Brush the gum arabic over the entire surface and leave to dry.

3 Quickly and evenly paint a second colour emulsion over the surface. Do not go over the same area more than once as this will mix and spoil the previously applied layers. Cracks start to appear very quickly — use a hair dryer to speed up the process and to make bigger cracks in the top layer of paint.

4 For a finer crackled finish, repeat steps 2 and 3. Finally, varnish or wax the surface to protect it from wear and tear.

Crackle varnish effect

Newly painted or restored items stand out harshly against those 'aged' by time. Methods have been evolved to copy the effects produced naturally over years, to lessen the contrast between old and new.

The first cracking varnish was patented by two French brothers in the 18th century. They discovered that by using varnishes with varying drying times — a quicker drying water-based varnish over a slower drying oil-based one — the top dry layer would crack as the lower layer moved while drying.

What to decorate

Crackle varnish can be used to age any paint-decorated surface, such as small items of furniture or picture frames. It also works well as a finish for découpaged objects.

Materials and equipment

Crackle varnish is available in a two-part pack, which contains two different varnishes. The slow-drying oil-based varnish is used first. The quicker drying water-based varnish is then brushed over the top. The pack is available from large art shops. You can make your own crackle varnish using an oil-based and water-based varnish. Experiment first, in case you do not achieve the required effect.

Artists' oils are rubbed into the surface to highlight the cracks. For an aged effect use dark, earthy colours like raw umber or burnt sienna. For a more modern look choose strong, bright colours.

The oil paint, mixed with a little white spirit, is rubbed lightly over the surface using a cloth. By going over the surface with a clean cloth excess paint can be removed, leaving a small amount in the cracks.

Crackle varnish method

You will need

◇ Crackle varnish pack (or two types of varnish: one oil-based and one water-based)
◇ Two paint brushes, about ½-1in (1.2-2.5cm) wide
◇ Artists' oils for highlighting the cracks
◇ White spirit
◇ Lint-free cotton rags

1 Thin first coat of varnish with white spirit, if necessary, so that you can brush it over the surface in a thin, very even layer. Leave to dry until the surface is just tacky when you touch it — this usually takes 1-2 hours, but can vary according to the temperature and humidity of the room you are working in.

2 Quickly cover the entire first coat of varnish with a thick layer of the second, water-based varnish. Leave to dry. The cracking becomes more obvious if you use a hair dryer to speed up the drying process.

▷ *This tray was painted and limed, and then 'aged' using the crackle varnish technique. The cracks were defined with artists' oil paints.*

3 When the varnish is dry, and if you are satisfied with the finish, continue to Step 4. If the cracking is too subtle, the first layer of varnish was too dry when the second coat was applied. In this case, wipe off the second varnish with a damp cloth and repeat steps 1 and 2, leaving less time between applying the coats.

4 Mix the chosen artists' oil colour with a little of the first coat of oil-based varnish. Using a rag, rub this gently over the entire surface and work it well into each of the cracks.

5 Using a clean, dry cloth, carefully remove the excess oil colour from the surface, leaving some in the cracks.

6 Allow final finish to dry for 3-7 days. Protect with two coats of oil-based varnish or wax.

Watercolour washes

*Transform a room by painting the furniture
in delicate pastel shades. These subtle effects are produced
using a watercolour paint wash — the colour gently
tints the furniture to give a translucent look. This easy
technique produces surprisingly stylish results.*

By co-ordinating the decor of a room, you can produce a feeling of balance and harmony. Here a folding screen, two stools, a chest of drawers, and various boxes and plates have been decorated with a paint wash using delicate pastel shades to produce an overall feeling of light and tranquillity.

The colour wash for the furniture is made by tinting inexpensive white emulsion paint, first diluted with water, with coloured inks or artists' watercolour paints. This makes it possible to make a wide range of coloured paint washes for the cost of just one tin of paint.

Experiment with colour

It is important to experiment with the colours you are going to use. This will enable you to make sure that each piece of furniture not only complements the others but also fits in with its surroundings.

An ideal and easy way to experiment with various colour combinations is to use paint sample colour charts, which are readily available from shops selling paints. Simply place different charts next to one another to see which colours work well together.

When planning the colour scheme, take into account the existing colours and patterns in the room. You could, for example, pick out some of the colours in a patterned settee or curtains. Or you might be inspired by the colours in a favourite picture or poster.

Materials and equipment

Little equipment is needed for these projects. Most of it, such as bowls, saucers and spoons for mixing paint, can be borrowed from the kitchen.

White water-based paint is used as the base ingredient for the colour wash. Water-based paints, such as emulsions, give a softer, more subtle effect than oil paints (which are much brighter and harder in tone because they reflect more light). To make the paint wash, a white matt emulsion is used as the base and diluted with a lot of water. Colour variations are then made by mixing pigments — in the form of gouache or inks — into the paint.

Gouache is an opaque, water-based paint which is sold in small tubes from artists' supply shops. It can be added to the diluted white paint emulsion to produce coloured washes.

Coloured inks are readily available from art shops and can be mixed with the diluted paint mixture in the same way as gouache to produce the colours of your choice. Coloured inks give a more translucent effect than gouache.

Making a paint wash

All water-based paints can be mixed with varying amounts of water so that they are thick and creamy or very runny. For the techniques shown here, you need to mix the paints to a very runny consistency. If the paint goes lumpy when you are mixing it, or forms a rubbery skin on the surface, you can remedy this by passing it through an ordinary large kitchen sieve.

Spend some time just experimenting with mixing colours; this will help you to achieve the exact shades you desire. It will also reveal any do's and don'ts of paint mixing and will help you judge the quantities of paint needed.

TIP ◆ **VARNISHING**

By their very nature, water-based paints are not waterproof. Therefore, any decorated surfaces which may come into contact with water — such as in a bathroom or kitchen — should be protected with a coat of matt glaze.

▽ *This studio apartment shows how it is possible to use a wide range of colours to decorate a room successfully. By carefully co-ordinating the tones and shades of a selection of colours, rather than just using a single colour, you can create a wonderfully tranquil and harmonious overall effect.*

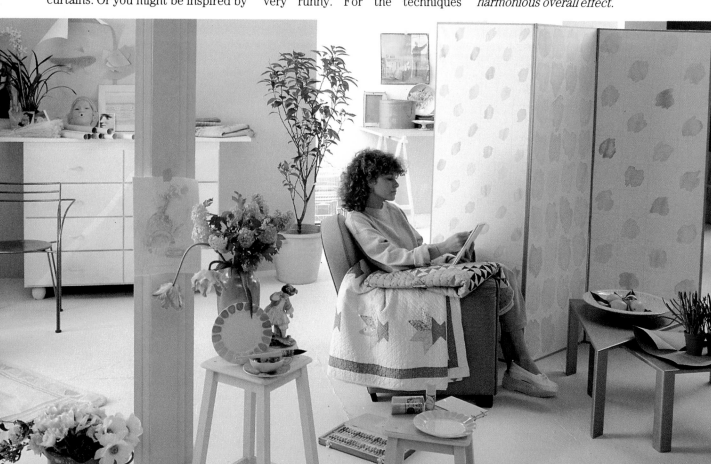

Pair of stools

The stools have been painted first with white matt emulsion and then a coloured wash. Use this method to paint any wooden items of furniture in your home — such as a small side table or a picture frame.

You will need
◇ White matt emulsion paint
◇ Water-based paints (either gouache or inks) in colours of your choice (we used bright red and cobalt blue)
◇ Sponge
◇ Spoon
◇ Matt varnish

Method

1 If necessary, prepare the surface of each stool before painting: sand them down using abrasive paper and then paint them with primer/undercoat. Sand them down again to remove any brush marks. Then paint each stool with a coat of undiluted white matt emulsion paint; sand down again to provide a smooth surface for the colour wash.

2 To make the basic watercolour paint wash, mix a small amount of white matt emulsion together with lots of water — as a rough guide, try adding 2tbsp of emulsion to each litre of water.

3 To produce a pastel tint, add a small amount of water-based paint (either gouache or ink) in a strong colour to some of the diluted paint mixture. Add only a few drops of colour at a time to each litre of diluted emulsion. Add the colour gradually for better control of the depth — it is easier to make a colour darker than it is to lighten it.

4 When you are happy with the pastel shade you have created, sponge the mixture on the stools using damp sponge (see pages 11-14).

5 Leave the tinted wash to dry completely. To protect the finish add a coat of matt varnish.

△ *While these stools have been painted for a practical use, the plates are purely decorative, giving you the opportunity to experiment with all your gouaches. (If you want to actually use these plates, you must use special ceramic paints.)*

Folding screen

Repeat the pastel theme by decorating an old screen to co-ordinate with the newly painted furniture. The screen is simply covered with a length of good quality water-colour paper, held in place with gummed paper sealing tape. The splashes of colour are added by painting an area of the paper with water, then adding a spot of gouache or ink, which diffuses to fill the area with soft colour.

Practise the technique first on remnant scraps of watercolour paper. Dampen and stretch the samples of paper before starting to paint.

You will need
◇ An old wooden folding screen
◇ A roll of thick watercolour paper
◇ Sponge
◇ Drawing pins
◇ Gummed paper sealing tape
◇ Ruler and pencil
◇ Watercolour paints or inks in the following colours: green, moss, lime, orange, grey and pink
◇ 1in (2.5cm) paint brush
◇ Blotting paper or absorbent cloth

Preparing the screen

1 From the roll of watercolour paper, cut a piece long enough to cover each panel. Dampen it with a very wet sponge or carefully soak it in a bath tub.

2 Once the paper is thoroughly dampened, smooth it over panel, making sure there are no air bubbles between paper and wood. Fix in place using drawing pins at corners and gummed craft paper round the edges of the wood. Leave to dry away from heat. It is important to soak and stretch the paper first to prevent it buckling when the paint wash is applied.

3 Draw a grid on to the paper, with each square measuring approximately 4in (10cm) across.

Painting the screen

1 Dip the paint brush into a beaker of water and paint patches of water well inside pencil grid.

2 Dip the brush into the first colour and dot it on one of the water spots. The colour will run and gradually diffuse through the water spot, making a slightly brighter colour round the edge. If necessary, use blotting paper or an absorbent cloth to soak up any excess moisture.

3 Repeat with the rest of the colours and allow to dry thoroughly away from any heat.

Chest of drawers

The chest has been painted with two washes — with a slash of white base coat left to divide the two colours. The handles are also painted in different pastel shades, chosen to complement the base colours.

You will need
◇ White matt undercoat
◇ White matt emulsion paint
◇ Gouache or ink (we used silver-grey and lilac)
◇ 2in (5cm) paint brush
◇ A sponge or lint-free cotton rag
◇ Masking tape
◇ Matt varnish

Method

1 If the chest has a wax finish, you should clean it with turpentine and then sand it before painting. Then paint the surface of the chest with matt white undercoat. Sand again to remove any brush marks.

2 Make up a diluted paint mixture, as for the stools (previous page, steps 2 and 3). Divide the mixture in half and make two separate pastel tints by adding the silver-grey to one and the lilac to the other.

△ *The pastel theme has been successfully repeated to decorate this folding screen. Although the screen has been divided with a very regular grid pattern, the actual splashes of colour on each section have been cleverly used to create different effects.*

3 Carefully position the masking tape diagonally across the front and top of the chest of drawers (refer to photograph) to divide the chest into two triangular sections.

4 Dip the paint brush into the pastel lilac wash, and brush it over the area to right hand side of masking tape. Do not take the wash right up to the tape, thus leaving slightly ragged edges.

5 Repeat this, using the silver-grey wash, to paint the area to the left of the masking tape, again stopping the wash just before the edge of the tape. Gently wipe over the finish with a rag or sponge. Use matt varnish to protect the surface.

◁ *Leave a slash of white between two soft pastel washes to prevent the colours from merging into one. A finishing coat of matt glaze will help to protect the surface from any splashes of water — especially when watering any plants being displayed on top!*

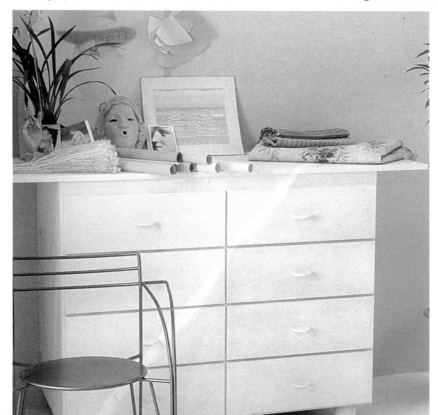

Combing

With its distinctive textured finish, combing is ideal for disguising shabby walls, furniture and wood. Although traditionally used to simulate woodgrain, this technique is now enjoying renewed popularity as a way of producing original patterns and colours on all sorts of surfaces.

This simple technique involves combing patterns into wet paint using a hard comb. A base coat is applied and allowed to dry. This is followed by a top coat which is combed while still wet so that the base coat shows through. The size and scale of the pattern is dictated by the size and spacing of the comb's teeth and to some extent by the material of the comb.

Combing is often referred to as a way of imitating or emphasizing the grain in woods. However, it can be quite difficult to re-create the natural, textured look of wood. The following few pages provide helpful, practical advice on the choice of combs available as well as demonstrating a variety of simple and more elaborate abstract combing designs that are much easier to achieve and are equally as effective.

Abstract combing

The strong lines produced by combing can also be used to create stripes, diagonals and patterns such as fans, waves and chequers in a wide variety of colours and interesting textures.

Some combing patterns can be used successfully on large surfaces; for example, dull floorboards can be livened up with a strong wavy pattern in a natural colour or, for real impact, in a bright and daring colour. Alternatively, small objects such as trays, boxes or frames can be given a more delicate combing decoration with the use of a fan or chequer technique.

◁ *Old furniture, such as this chest of drawers, can find new favour with the addition of cheerful and original textured patterns. The chest was bought in a junk shop and combed in dramatic black on a white undercoat.*

Materials and equipment
Paints

Base coat On walls, the base colour for a combed surface can either be emulsion or an oil-based undercoat. On furniture and floors, use an oil-based undercoat.

Top coat The combed colour should be an oil-based paint such as gloss or eggshell. This is slow drying and remains workable long enough for you to make the combed textures and patterns. You can also use thinned artist's oil colours — although these are quite expensive and very slow drying. Better still, a scumble glaze (a translucent oil-based glaze available from specialist shops) tinted with artist's oil colours provides a transparent combing colour which allows the ground colour to show through and adds another dimension to the finished effect.

To ensure a workable consistency your paint should be diluted with white spirit (up to 25 per cent), but remember that the paint must be thick enough to hold the texture of the combed marks.

Varnish

When the combed paint is dry it is possible to apply added protection to the finish with a matt or gloss varnish. If you have used a gloss oil-based paint for the combed surface it is only necessary to varnish if the surface is to be subjected to the excessive wear and tear that might be expected in a bathroom or kitchen.

However, gloss varnish can be used as an additional decorative element which can give lift to the colours beneath the glassy surface.

Rubber comb

Afro comb

DIY serrated spatulas

Cardboard comb

Woodgraining combs

Combs

A flexible comb is used to make patterns; rigid materials can be used, but take care not to scrape and damage the base colour.

Wood-graining combs These are usually made of rubber and come in a range of sizes. Some rubber combs have graduated teeth which produce a series of lines with varying widths and spaces.

Triangular combs are also available, which have the advantage of combining three different spacing options in one implement.

Steel woodgraining combs These must be covered with a thin, lint-free cloth before they are pulled over the paint surface.

DIY spatulas Use the flexible plastic serrated type that comes with adhesives and fillers.

Hair combs Afro combs are effective because they have chunky, widely spaced teeth.

Alternatively, cut your own comb from stiff cardboard and seal it with a coat of varnish. A coarser comb can be cut from a work tile.

Preparing surfaces

Plaster walls, lining paper, wooden floors and furniture are all suitable for combing. It is not possible, however, to comb woodchip or other papers with a raised pattern. New or unpainted wood should be primed before applying a base coat and new plaster should be left for at least six months to dry out before priming. Rub down painted woodwork and fill any holes or cracks.

On uneven walls, the combed colour and texture tends to be irregular. However, this can look attractive and be effective over a large area.

Combing surfaces

1 Apply an even base coat to the prepared surface. Leave to dry, then rub down lightly and repeat if necessary.

2 Thin the top colour slightly with white spirit (if it is too thick, you will get ugly, uneven ridges in the pattern) and brush over the base. Remember, once the paint starts to dry it cannot be combed, so work a manageable area at a time.

3 When using a fairly transparent paint (or glaze) there may be faint brush marks in the surface. On large areas these will not show; on small items you can remove them before combing by lightly dabbing the wet paint with a soft cloth.

4 Drag the comb through the wet surface to reveal the contrasting colour of the base coat beneath, keeping your strokes as even as possible. You can vary the pattern by changing the direction of your strokes (see overleaf).

5 Once you are happy with the pattern and have applied the desired layers of combing, it is important to leave the paint until it is completely dry. If necessary apply two thin coats of clear varnish to protect the textured surface.

Fan shapes

Of all the methods of combing that can be used, these fan shapes produce possibly the most dramatic, textured effect, particularly on smaller objects, as can be seen with this simple tray (below). The pattern is created by keeping one end of the comb in the same position and swivelling the other end around to form an arc (right). Further overlapping rows of arcs are then applied.

Colour schemes

Choice of colour will make all the difference to the final design. In order to achieve the right effect, the base colour should be of a contrasting tone to the intended top coat colour. In other words, if your combed colour is to be dark, choose a white or pale base. Conversely, use a dark base under a light coloured top coat.

For the more adventurous, it is possible to introduce subsequent colours into a combed design. This can be done by applying a second colour over the first and superimposing another combed pattern — in which case, the second colour will dominate. Alternatively, you can introduce random splashes of top coat colours on the first combing.

◆ TIP	TRIAL RUN

Try out your paint first and experiment with the amount of white spirit you will need. The absorbency of the surface, the type of paint, even the weather will affect the way the paint can be worked.

PATTERN LIBRARY

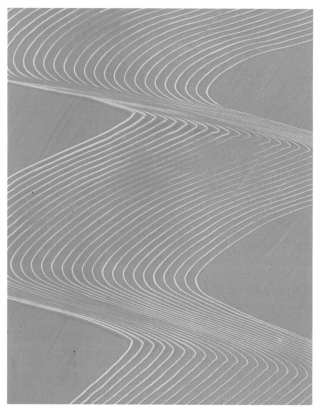

Criss-cross zigzag A comb with graduated teeth is used to pull abstract zigzag patterns on top of one another, vertically and horizontally.

Waves Undulating and waving lines can be used on a large area, such as a floor surface, or as borders and edging patterns.

Fine criss-cross This is an easy way of creating a fabric-like effect on any surface. All you do is work horizontally and vertically with a fine comb.

Zigzag Pulling the comb backwards and forwards diagonally, changing direction sharply at each edge, creates an angular, zigzag pattern.

Using wood stains

Staining timber can bring out or improve the richness of a wood's natural colour as well as enhancing the pattern of the grain. Newer semi-translucent paints widen the palette to include a rainbow of bright and pastel colours not seen in natural timber.

Wood stains are now available in a wide range of colours, opening up a whole world of decorative effects. By carefully choosing the right type of wood stain it is possible to transform the appearance of a timber floor or a piece of furniture to give them subtle colour. It is also possible to give cheaper softwoods the appearance of more expensive hardwoods with stains in wood tones.

Wood stains can also be used to create a range of more unusual effects. You can, for example, stain different sections of a piece of furniture to create tonal contrasts or stain floorboards to mimic beautiful, more costly woods.

Stunning effects can be created by using semi-transparent colour stains that allow the natural grain of the wood to show through. You can give floors and traditional wooden furniture soft, pastel tints or use brighter co-ordinating colours to make patchwork effects or striped designs on smaller wooden items.

Staining timber floors

An expanse of timber floor provides a canvas for original designs and colour use. Floorboards can be painted in stripes and plain wood panels can be transformed with a patchwork of pastel stains.

If the timber is in poor condition, or you have concrete floors, cover the existing floor with ply squares, mosaic panels or strip flooring. These can then be stained.

Staining furniture

Traditional timber furniture is brought to life by staining. Even old pine furniture that has been stripped can benefit from the addition of a golden stain to bring back its warmth. New pine can be stained to blend with old timber doors and skirtings, and existing pine furniture.

Skirtings and doors

Use a pastel-coloured translucent stain to match skirtings and doors to walls that are painted or papered in soft colours. Alternatively, harmonize the decor of a room by staining floorboards, skirtings and doors in the same shade so that they will blend together beautifully.

Garden furniture

If you intend to stain furniture that remains outdoors it is important to choose a stain, varnish or seal designed for outdoor use. Microporous stains that contain a fungicide to protect the finish against mould

▽ *Floorboards can be painted in stripes, or you can create tonal effect by staining sections of floor with pastel or primary stains.*

△ *Traditional wooden furniture can be given a new lease of life by staining. Prepare the surface by removing any existing paint or varnish finish and sanding the surface to remove any marks or scratches in the wood. Try using a stain with a faint hint of colour to add a warm natural glow to the item of furniture.*

growth and an ultra-violet filter that acts against bleaching by the sun are ideal for garden furniture. This finish will be quite matt. If you want a high shine to your furniture apply a varnish designed for outdoor use over the wood stain.

Materials and equipment

Apart from the stain itself you need surprisingly little equipment to stain wood. Buy some sandpaper to pre-pare the surface of the wood before you start work. A good quality brush or clean cloth is also essential so that you can apply the stain, and you may need a thinner to thin down the stain you decide to use.

Stains

Wood stains fall into two main types — those that stain the wood but give no protection to the surface, and those that are mixed with varnish so that the wood is both coloured and protected at the same time.

Stain on its own This type of stain does not give any protection to the wood, so the surface will need prot-ection by polish or oil. It is therefore specially suitable for renovating old furniture. The stain can be thinned using white spirit for spirit-based stains or water for water-based stains.

This type of stain dries quickly which can make it difficult to apply evenly. Working along the grain, apply the stain sparingly with a cloth. Do not go over an area that has already been covered with stain or the finish will become blotchy. When the finish is dry, oil or polish it.

Varnish stain This type of stain colours and protects the wood at the same time. Each coat of varnish slightly deepens the colour. Apply a number of layers of stain for a deep colour. If you want more protection but no greater depth of colour, finish off with a clear varnish instead.

Varnish stains can be poly-urethane or acrylic based. Poly-urethane-based varnish is available in a satin or gloss finish, and will need to be thinned with white spirit. Leave up to 12 hours drying time bet-ween coats. Acrylic-based varnish is available only in a satin finish and must be thinned before use with water. A coat of acrylic varnish takes only 30 minutes to dry and can be re-coated in two hours.

All-in-one wood stain and prot-ective finish is also available. This is oil-based and it dries quickly. This means it can be re-coated in two hours time. It is available in a gloss or satin finish. Some brands are sold in a tester size so you can try out the colour.

Colourful wood finishes Unlike opaque paint, semi-translucent col-oured finishes still allow the grain of the wood to show through. They are oil-based and are brushed on to give a protective satin finish. You can choose from pastel shades or more vibrant colours. If a matt or gloss fin-ish is required, clear varnish can be used on top of the stain.

Brushes Choose a good quality brush and use it only for varnishing. Dislodge any loose bristles before starting work, and clean the brush well after use so that it can be used again for the next project.

Cloth On curved and moulded wood it is easier to achieve an even finish with a cloth than with a brush. For this method use a cloth which is soft, clean and lint free.

Preparing the wood

Wood that is to be stained needs care-ful preparation beforehand as any irregularities, marks or stains will be obvious once the wood stain is app-lied. Previously untreated, lightly col-oured wood shows off colour best, but older surfaces can come up well if they are prepared properly.

Remove all paint or varnish from wood before applying wood stain. Fill any holes, dents and scratches with wood filler or stopping and sand the surface down to ensure a smooth finish. For sanding floors hire a large commercial sander and a smaller edging sander. Seal any bleeding knots in the timber with knotting, and seal open-grained wood with grain filler. If you want to lighten wood use a proprietry wood bleach. This has the added advan-tage of removing any surface stains.

Test wood stain on a spare piece of the same wood or in a hidden area of the item to be stained before you start. You can then be certain of what the finished result will look like and make any changes necessary.

▽ *Coloured wood finishes still allow the natural grain of the wood to show through. The pastel green translucent wood stain used on this chest of drawers looks very pretty and you could always try staining skirting boards and doors to match. The tasselled knobs add a decorative touch.*

◁ *Here a red and green varnish has been applied to alternate floor panels with the third panel coated with a natural varnish for a pleasing contrast. By treating the panels in different colours, a strong pattern is formed.*

Staining a plant trough

Show off the decorative design of a timber plant trough by highlighting its shape and pattern with a range of deep pastel, translucent paint stains. The colour scheme you choose for the trough should complement the colours of any other surfaces around it, and you can plant flowers and shrubs to blend in with the scheme.

You will need

◇ Translucent paint stain in three colours
◇ ½in (1cm) and 1½in (3cm) decorators' brushes
◇ Masking tape
◇ Thick, clear plastic sheeting
◇ Double the area of the box base with an extra 2in (5cm) on all sides to allow for overlap
◇ Enough grit or small pebbles to cover the base to a depth of ¾in (2cm).

1 Sand new wood to a smooth finish, fill any holes with wood filler and apply knotting to knots to prevent bleeding. On dark wood the colours will be less clear, so you may wish to lighten the timber first using a wood bleach. Remove any existing paint or varnish from old wood.

2 First surround the outer panels of the box with masking tape to avoid any of the colour used for the box lining appearing on the outside. Also mask the leg edges on the outer frame where the green stained frame abuts them. Press down the tape lightly but firmly so that no stain can seep underneath.

▽ *This attractive wooden plant trough will make a welcome addition to any garden.*

3 Using the larger brush apply the green stain sparingly to the inside of the box, brushing in the direction of the wood grain. Stain the trellis areas of the outer container, using the smaller brush in the same way. Leave to dry. For a stronger colour you can apply a second coat, but leave the first to dry overnight. Remove the tape before the stain is completely dry.

4 When the stain is dry, apply more masking tape along the green stained top edge of the box then stand this upside down on supports to hold it above the working surface. Mask all the green stained edges adjacent to the legs of the frame and stand this on small supports too.

5 Working with the wood grain, brush the pink stain on to the outer sides and underneath of the inner panels. Then use blue stain to coat the four legs of the outer container. Leave to dry. Recoat if necessary and remove tape.

6 When the box is completely dry, line with plastic sheeting. Cut the plastic in half and line the box so that the sheeting comes equally 2in (5cm) up all four sides. Add a ¾in (2cm) layer of grit or small pebbles to the base of the box before placing plants in their pots in position.

TIP   A TROUGH

You can make a similar, but simpler, decorative trough. Just cut wooden garden trellis to fit all four sides of a large, rectangular timber box. Stain the box and trellis separately. When both are dry, glue the trellis in position and secure with screws. If necessary, touch up the trough with more coloured stain.

A row of three or four basic, square timber boxes — the type normally used as rustic plant containers — will also look effective when stained. Use a selection of pastel colours to create a harmonious combination.

Scumbling

*The paint effect known as scumbling, or
scrumbling, involves using glaze and paint to tone and merge
colours on a surface. The glaze is designed to
remain wet and workable long enough to enable you to apply
the colour and create decorative finishes.*

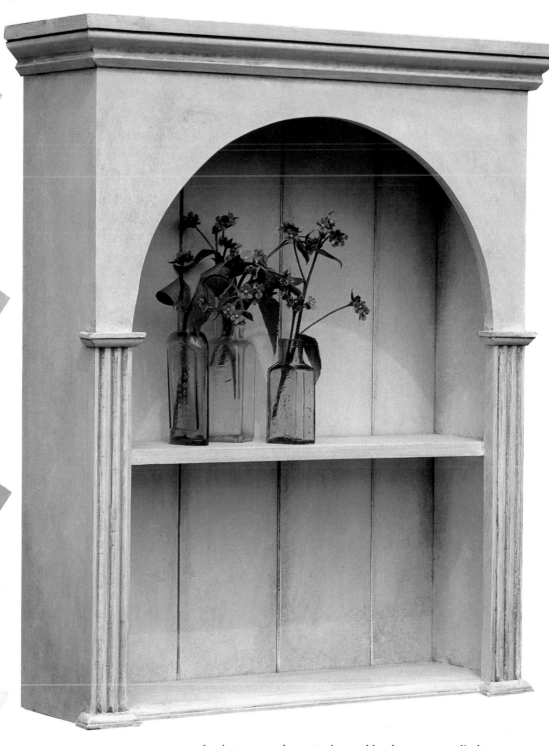

△ *A green and mustard scumble glaze was applied to
the off-white base coat of this shelf. The samples show
some other possible colour effects.*

Scumbling is a quick and easy paint technique which mixes wet paint and oil glaze over a dry base colour. Oil glaze, then oil paint, is brushed on to a surface. While it is still wet, some of the paint and glaze mixture is wiped away with a clean, soft, lint-free cloth. The colours are then blended and toned to achieve the desired effect.

The important thing to remember with this technique is that you must work quickly, before the oil glaze becomes too dry.

Adding highlights

Scumbling works especially well on furniture with ornamental details. It can be used to highlight certain areas and add shadows to others.

This paint technique can also be used to add shape and dimension to large, flat surfaces. This is done by using two different shades of the base coat — one slightly lighter and one slightly darker. Use the darker shade in the corners and edges furthest away from the light source and the lighter shade in the centre and edges closest to light.

Preparation

Whatever item you choose to paint must be prepared before decorating. Scumbling accentuates cracks and crevices, so make sure you scumble only those surface marks you want to focus on. Remove peeling or flaking paint and fill in cracks and surface flaws. Then sand and prime with an appropriate oil-based primer.

Apply two coats of the base colour, lightly sanding between each coat. Use an oil-based paint with a matt finish, as scumbling will slide on a semi-gloss or gloss surface. Once second coat is dry, lightly sand and wipe with a damp cloth.

You will need
◇ Oil-based primer
◇ Oil-based base coat, matt finish (we used an off-white colour)
◇ Transparent oil glaze (sometimes called scumble glaze)
◇ Household oil-based paint (we used blue-green and mustard)
◇ Three 1in (2.5cm) or 2in (5cm) natural bristled paint brushes (one for the glaze and one for each paint colour to be scumbled)
◇ Lots of soft, lint-free rags (cheesecloth or mutton cloth)
◇ White spirit
◇ Sandpaper

Method

1 Prepare and prime the surface. Apply two coats of the base colour. (See 'Preparation').

2 Liberally apply the oil glaze to the base coat. Work on just a small area at a time to enable you to apply the colour and wipe it away before the glaze dries. (The glaze remains wet and workable for about 20 minutes).

3 Brush the oil-based paint on top of the glaze. Apply the blue-green colour to the shadows and recesses in the moulding. Add the mustard colour to the flat surface and to the relief areas of the moulding. Apply the paint as broadly or as gently as you like, but make sure you leave some of the base coat showing.

4 Wipe off some of the paint and glaze with a rag to reveal more of the base coat and blend and soften the colours. Whenever the cloth becomes clogged with paint and glaze, replace with a fresh cloth. Soften the surface more, either by dabbing with a soft cloth or by stippling with a natural bristled brush.

5 Once you have achieved the desired effect, allow the surface to dry and then protect it with an oil-based varnish.

Dry scumbling

The paint technique of dry scumbling involves
lightly dry-brushing four to six varying shades of the
same colour on to a surface. This method allows
tiny flecks of the different shades to show through,
creating a soft, mottled appearance.

Dry scumbling is an excellent paint technique for giving newly painted pieces of furniture, walls and doors the mellow appearance of age. This fairly easy technique can be used to match new furniture to older items, or simply for the pleasure of the striking, yet subtle, textured effect which can be achieved.

Preparation

Furniture needs to be properly prepared and primed. When dry scumbling interior walls, it is best to work directly on to the primed plaster, as this will enhance the texture of the paint effect. Walls painted in warm earth tones, such as yellow ochre or burnt sienna, take on the appearance of a fresco.

For interior walls

Scrape away loose, chipped paint and fill and sand any surface imperfections and cracks. Raw plaster should be primed with a water-based primer. Make sure that previously painted walls are completely dust free and clean before you dry scumble them.

◁ *Tones of one colour are layered, starting with lightest tone.*

▽ *These stencilled details were added after the third layer of paint had been applied.*

For furniture

Items of furniture should be prepared following the instructions in the previous scumbling article, but using a water-based undercoat or primer rather than an oil-based one. While major surface cracks and flaws should be filled, minor imperfections add to the textured effect of this paint technique. Use your judgement to decide which to fill and which to leave as character. For more information, see pages 47-48.

Paint mixing

For a successful finish, various shades of one colour need to be mixed separately. To do this, pour small amounts of white emulsion into individual containers; then add varying amounts of the chosen colour to each and stir well to give four to six different shades of colour. If the shades look too similar, add more white or more of the chosen colour.

Small amounts of a different colour can be added to one or two of the shades to tint them slightly further. Raw or burnt umber 'age' a shade while brighter colours, such as yellow or orange, add a lively hue. Do not be afraid to experiment with one of the shades, as the layering method only allows flecks of each colour to show through.

Dry scumbling

You will need

◇ White, water-based household emulsion paint to act as the base for mixing the different shades
◇ Water-based household emulsion paint in the colour of your choice
◇ 1-2in (2.5-5cm) natural bristle brush for painting furniture or 3-4in (7.5-10cm) natural bristle brush for painting walls
◇ 4-6 containers for mixing the various tints or shades used for the dry scumbling
◇ Newspaper
◇ Fine grade abrasive paper

Method

1 Prepare and prime the surface. Mix the paints, as described opposite in 'Paint mixing'.

2 Using the lightest shade, paint a base coat over the entire primed surface. Leave it to dry thoroughly and then gently sand with fine grade abrasive paper, so that a little of the primed surface shows through. Wipe away the dust with a slightly damp cloth.

4 At this point the surface might look blotchy, but do not worry as the overall effect is achieved by building up a number of layers. Continue working, lightly and dryly, from light to dark paint, allowing flecks of previously painted colours to show through. Allow each colour to dry before proceeding to the next.

3 Working from the lightest shade to the darkest, take the next shade in the sequence and apply it, lightly and dryly. To do this, dip the brush into the paint and remove the excess paint by brushing on to a piece of newspaper. Do not allow your brush to become heavily laden with paint. Start painting, varying the direction of your brush stroke, from side to side and up and down. The idea is that you do not completely cover the base coat, allowing spots and patches of the previous coat to show through. Leave each coat of paint to dry before applying the next layer.

TIP ◇	DECORATIVE FEATURES

For a more authentic look, extra decorative features, such as the stencilled design on the wash stand door in this chapter, should be added before applying the last scumbled layer.

5 As you apply your third and fourth colours the brush strokes will disappear and the effect will start to look soft and mottled. The successive layers of paint build up an interesting texture which you can actually feel. Continue adding layers of paint until you have worked your way through all of the colours. When finished, leave to dry completely.

Finishing off

It is not essential to seal walls after they have been dry scumbled. If necessary, they can be kept clean by gently and carefully washing them with warm soapy water. Major marks or scratches can be quickly touched up by scumbling over them.

Furniture can be protected with two coats of matt or semi-gloss polyurethane varnish. However, it is not necessary to varnish the items: as with the walls, areas can be touched up by scumbling over them; alternatively, for a more distressed, aged look, worn areas can be left as they are.

Creating an aged look

The effects given by dry scumbling can be taken a step further, to achieve a more antique look, using a technique known as distressing. This involves applying layers of paint or varnish — in the same way as for dry scumbling — but gently sanding between the layers to remove some of the colour. For a professional, yet subtle, finish it is best to combine dry scumbling with other effects such as antiquing or distressing.

Some people go to even greater lengths to give furniture an authentically aged look. Keys, chains and even bricks can be bashed against or dropped on to areas of the furniture to give an appearance of general wear and tear. But this must be done very subtly, as it is easy to overdo it: look at genuinely old items to see which parts have been naturally worn, such as handles, or corners of drawers or table tops which people have handled over many years.

If further decorative details are to be applied, these should also be given a look of age. New gilding can be made dull by coating it with a solution of burnt umber gouache mixed with a little water and a drop of detergent. Decorative lining or stencilled designs can be gently rubbed away in places to make them more in keeping with the piece.

△ This new cabinet was given a distressed paint effect to make it look like a period piece.

◁ Small repairs were carried out on this old blanket box, then its' age was enhanced with distressing.

◁ A Tyrolean painted coffer, dated 1800, shows the true beauty of a paint effect that has mellowed and worn with time. It is just this type of effect that the modern distressed paint techniques aim to emulate.

Marbling

*The rich effect of marble is surprisingly easy to imitate.
By using the appropriate type of paint and the right equipment,
you can create small panels of marble to decorate
accessories or furniture, or even use the technique to
cover larger areas, such as doors or walls.*

The fantasy effect

Marble is a luxurious material, rarely used in its natural form these days except for small areas — tiles, fireplaces and accessories such as boxes and lamp bases are the most common examples. In history, it was used more extravagantly in grand households, for floors and even walls. It is an expensive material and difficult to handle, so it makes sense to have a bit of fun and develop your colour skills to imitate the effect.

Surfaces for marbling

For a true-to-life effect, apply the finish to the type of surface where you might find the real thing.

Wooden boxes and fire surrounds, panels along the dado, beneath a chair rail, or even a panelled door. Wooden floors — stripped floorboards, floors levelled with chipboard or plywood, or prepared concrete floors — can look particularly effective with a marbled finish, especially if they are painted to imitate tiles. However, they will need extra protection over the paint to prevent rapid wear.

Try to reproduce a natural effect by observing marble as it is actually used: the size of panels of marble is limited because of the weight of the material. It is unusual to find large panels — large areas are usu-

ally clad in several smaller panels, often arranged to create a pattern. The weight also affects where it is used. Permanent fixtures, for example, skirting boards, are realistic situations for marble. Marble doors or windows would be impossibly heavy, but if it is a fantasy effect you are after, the paint finish is a practical option.

Colour and tone

Look at the natural variations of colour and the veining effect in real marble. You will find examples on existing fireplaces, and in particular as a facing material on commercial buildings.

Artist's oil paints

Lint-free rag

Universal stainers

Household paint brush

Badger hair brush

Round brush

Feathers

Scumble glaze

Sponge

Artist's brushes

Materials and equipment

Paints

Ordinary household paints cannot be used on their own to create a marbled paint effect. There are some specialist materials which you will need.

Scumble glaze is an oil-based, translucent paint medium, rather like varnish. It is used for many paint effects, because it has what is known as 'a long open time'. This means that it takes a long time to dry, so you can work it, adding colour which sinks into the surface, without bleeding into it. The glaze has no pigment, so that even if you add colour (in the form of oil-based household or artist's paints), successive coats have a translucence, allowing base colours to show through.

Household paints are used for the base coat and also to tint the glaze. Use only oil-based paints (in the form of gloss and eggshell paint) which will mix with the scumble glaze. The colours you use will depend on the marble you are

In most types of marble, an all-over mottled effect is interrupted by veins and variations in the density or tone of colour. The effect is imitated by mixing carefully graduated tones of paint and building up a base colour. While this coat is still wet, the 'veins' in another colour are added. Before the paint dries, the whole effect can be softened by brushing over the surface.

The natural lustre of marble is only evident when the stone is cut and polished. When painting imitation marble, this polish is created by adding coats of glaze, rather like varnish, so that the colour sinks beneath the surface.

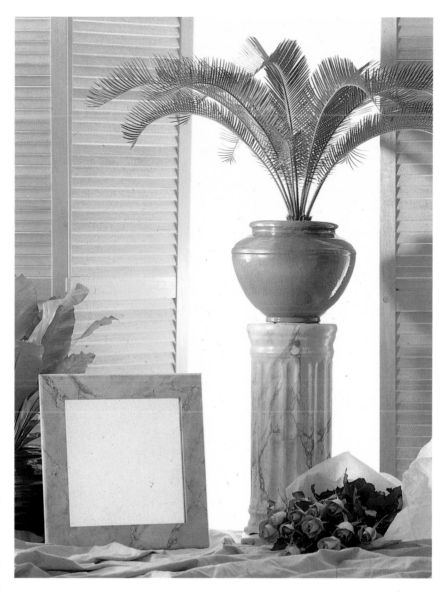

trying to imitate — creamy whites, palest greys, or rich dark greens, even pinks and reds.

Universal stainers can be used to tint the base coat, if the colour you want is not available, or to create subtle variations in tone. They can also be used to tint the glaze and are particularly effective when you want to add colour without detracting from its translucence, in order to build up the 'polish' of marble.

Artist's oil paints can also be used to tint both the base coat and subsequent glaze coats. However, their main use is to paint in veins of colour. Traditional shades to use are burnt sienna and dark grey on pale marble; white and green on black backgrounds, and so on. It is always worth having some white paint to hand to add body to colours and for extra emphasis when painting in veins.

White spirit is used to thin the coats of colour. Suggested proportions for mixing are given on the following page. Mixing white spirit with artist's oil paint before adding it to paint or glaze makes it easier to blend.

Brushes
Household paint brushes should be of good quality. Use clean brushes, which are free of dust and do not shed hairs. The size depends on the surface you are painting: for small items, a ½in (12mm) brush may be adequate; for walls or floors you will need a 4in (10cm) brush for the main part of the surface and a 1in (2.5cm) brush for corners that are difficult to get to.

Artist's brushes are used for painting in details. Stiff, round brushes are useful for stippling background colour. Softer, broad brushes can be used to add variations in tone, and soft, fine brushes are best for adding veins. Build up a collection of brushes, and experiment with the different effects they give.

Feathers are often used by professionals for softening the veins — or even for painting them in. If you are tackling a large area, make sure you have several feathers of similar weight, as they tend to get clogged with paint and are easily damaged.

Sponges and rags can be used at various stages in the work to create mottled patterns.

Clean soft brushes can also be used to soften the effect professional decorators use long soft brushes of badger hair, but you can also use large artist's brushes or even make-up brushes as long as they do not shed hairs.

△ *With every layer of glaze, veins and mottling that you add, so the surface you are decorating takes on the cool distinction of marble. The pale marble effect that has been applied to this mirror and plinth gives them a new distinction that is easy to imitate.*

Applying the colours

In order to create individual colours and a workable medium, it is always necessary to experiment before tackling a job. The type of surface you are painting, the brushes and equipment you use and the brand of paint you buy are all part of the finished effect — even the weather can affect the outcome.

Start with a well-prepared surface, free from splinters or flaking paint. Seal with undercoat if it is porous. You must start with an evenly absorbent surface.

Choose and mix a colour for the base coat — you can usually use a standard household colour. The undercoat may be sufficient.

For the next coat, mix a glaze. This may be tinted with any of the types of paint described on the previous pages — add household eggshell paint for a more opaque colour, or just universal stainers if you want the colour beneath to show through.

Adding texture and tone

After applying the glaze, work in variations of tone to the background colour, by dabbing on artist's oil paint or tinted eggshell paint. Use brushes, sponges — even rags — to break up the colour of the base coat.

Next, add a structure of veins across the surface, using an artist's paint brush. Again, you can use artist's oils or tints of eggshell, with or without glaze. While the paint is still wet, soften the lines as necessary, using a feather or soft brush. When doing this, always work in one direction, to keep a hard edge along one side of the veins and a faded effect along the other.

You can build up variations in tone and add extra depth to the surface by adding further coats of glaze, mixed fairly thin and lightly tinted with colour. As you build up successive coats, the veins will sink beneath the surface.

Mixing glazes

For an opaque glaze, good proportions to work with are three parts oil-based scumble, five parts off-white eggshell and 2 parts white spirit. Mix the paint with the glaze, then add the white spirit to give a creamy consistency.

For a more translucent glaze, tint the glaze with oil paints or stainers, then add a roughly equal quantity of white spirit.

Pale marbling effect

You can create many interesting tonal effects using pale colours. Here varying shades of grey have been used, a hint of umber adds a realistic finishing touch.

You will need

◇ Undercoat or eggshell paint (dependent on surface)
◇ Artist's oil paints in umber and varying shades of grey
◇ Translucent glaze
◇ Household paint brushes
◇ Soft, flat artist's brush
◇ Soft make-up brush
◇ Natural sponge
◇ Lint-free rags
◇ Glasspaper
◇ White spirit

1 Rub down the surface to be decorated and apply undercoat (on wood or metal) or eggshell (on walls) in a suitable colour. The paint effect will look better if you take care over this stage.

2 If necessary, apply a further coat to act as a base coat for the decorative finish. Tint it slightly with grey oil paint, and use a sponge to create lightly mottled areas.

3 Using mid-grey artist's oil and an artist's brush, start to create a random trellis of diagonal veins across the surface.

4 Strengthen some of the veins with darker colours, then soften the effect by brushing over the surface with a soft brush.

5 Use a natural sponge to create variations in tone, lifting off colour or applying extra colour where needed.

6 Apply a translucent glaze, with a light umber tint. In some patches, add extra coats of glaze for a natural effect.

Bambooing

*Imitating the natural look of bamboo brings
a stylish feel to previously uninspiring furniture. By
taking the technique one step further, and using
colours from your imagination, the fantasy effect created can range
from the sophisticated to the surreal.*

Unlike paint effects such as sponging and rag-rolling, which bring texture and interest to decorations and furniture, fantasy effects create something altogether different. They take a surface or object and change our perception of it. A plain, wooden floor can take on the grandiose feel of marble; a dull picture frame is given the luxury of tortoiseshell; an uninspiring room is made to look quite grand with antiquing and gliding.

Bambooing, despite being fairly intricate, is perhaps the easiest fantasy effect to take on, adding individuality to tired furnishings.

▽ *The staircase at the Brighton Pavilion reflects the interest in oriental styles.*

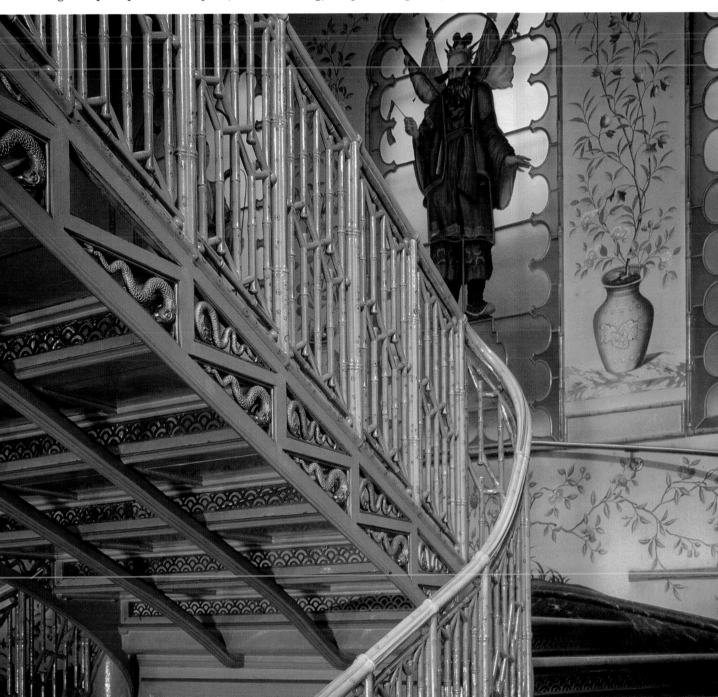

What is bambooing?

Bambooing was developed in the eighteenth century in response to the passion among the upper classes for all things oriental.

Bambooing is a fine technique that can use natural colours to imitate the look of real bamboo or artificial colours for an unreal fantasy effect. The bands and knots of natural bamboo are reproduced, usually in unrealisitic colours. It is most convincing when used on light pieces of furniture such as chairs, tables and plant stands.

Bamboo effects can be applied to normal wood, although plaster of Paris may be used to alter the shape of the wood for even greater authenticity. The best 'unreal' effects are achieved on pieces of furniture made from natural bamboo. During the height of its popularity, the technique was applied to furnishings and fittings carved or cast to look like bamboo: the staircase of Brighton's Pavilion, built in the nineteenth century, is a renowned example.

▽ *The shapes, sizes and details of real bamboo provide a fine natural example of how anything goes when creating a bamboo effect.*

The look of bamboo

The actual detail of the bamboo can be added in various ways. The effect to aim for is bands of graduated colour at each of the ring-joints of the bamboo (you will have to decide where to position these if you are not using natural bamboo or bamboo-turned wood). Running down the length of the bamboo, tapering V-shapes from the ring-joints are painted to represent the spines of the bamboo, while small knots or 'eyes' are randomly dotted over the surface of the wood, fairly close to the spines.

Materials and equipment
Paints

Base coat This must have a matt finish, and be oil-based for durability. You can simply use several layers of undercoat for the base coat or, for the best results, finish the undercoat with an oil-based eggshell paint.

Top coat Traditionally, oil-based glaze was used, mixed with eggshell paint to give a certain opacity, and tinted with artist's oil paints or universal stainers. More paint was added to create progressively darker and more opaque mixtures for the bamboo details.

It is not essential to use the traditional scumble glaze to create the effect, as artist's oils mixed with varnish produce a similar result. However, the most convenient paints to use are artist's acrylics, thinned with water. It is much easier to achieve fantasy effects with these colours, which have the advantage of being quick drying, so you can paint the shades in a matter of hours.

Varnish

Whatever paint you use it is necessary to give the item two or three coats of silk or gloss polyurethane varnish to protect against accidental damage and wear and tear. Low sheen varnish is better for paler tones, but if you use oriental blacks, jades and golds you will need a gloss varnish to create a lacquered effect.

Brushes

Regular decorator's paint brushes or flat, soft-bristled artist's brushes can be used for the base coat and the bamboo effect bands. You will need a clean brush for varnishing. The greater detail of the rings, spines and eyes requires a number 1 and finer brushes.

The bamboo shape

To enhance the fantasy effect it is possible to add shape to a plain piece of wood by using plaster of Paris. Make up a fairly liquid plaster of Paris mixture and use your finger to apply a little to the wood at the point where you want the ring to be. This can be rather fiddly, but the plaster dries quickly so you can build up the ridge using several layers. Then carve the plaster with a craft knife and rub down with glasspaper. Prime both the plaster and wood prior to decoration.

Preparing the surface

If you are using bamboo that has not been decorated before but has been polished, rub down with fine wire wool and methylated spirits. This is particularly important with wax polish, which will prevent the paint from taking. Rub down previously painted items with fine glasspaper.

Prime any bare wood so that it is ready to take a coat of paint. Alternatively you can use a dual purpose primer/undercoat. Ensure that you have all the right brushes to hand. You will need a small container in which to mix your colours.

1 Apply at least three layers of base coat, rubbing down well between coats: for a particularly fine, smooth finish, rub down with wet-and-dry paper that has been dipped in soapy water. If you have decided to use eggshell for the top layer of the base coat, allow the paint to dry and then rub down lightly to reduce the sheen.

2 If you are not using natural bamboo, decide on the positions for the rings and mark the centre of each ring in pencil. The rings are usually about 6in (15cm) apart and can be evenly or unevenly spaced. Using a pale acrylic paint and a ⅝in (1.5cm) brush, paint a 2in (5cm) band round the bamboo. Repeat until all the rings are complete, and allow to dry.

3 Using a slightly darker and less translucent paint mixture, add a second band of colour inside the first about ⅝in (1.5cm) wide. Even when working on a straight surface, the combination of this and the lighter band creates a contoured appearance. Repeat for each band and allow to dry.

4 Using the darkest tone of paint, pick out the notch line around the ring of the bamboo with a number 1 artist's brush. At the same time, using the same tone but a number 00 artist's brush, pick out fine V-shaped spines running from the rings along a third of the length of the individual bamboo section.

5 Plan the position of the 'eyes' carefully — one or two fairly close to each spine will be plenty. Using the artist's brushes, apply a blob of pale or mid-tone paint followed by a tiny dot in the centre and two or three further dots in the darkest tone.

6 When you are happy with the effect and the paint is completely dry, apply at least three coats of either silk or gloss polyurethane protective varnish, depending on the finish you wish to create. Rub down lightly with glasspaper between coats.

DESIGN LIBRARY

The colours you choose for the bamboo effect depend on the overall effect desired, and the decor of the room. For a natural bamboo look choose pale yellow ochre or sienna for the base coat, adding rings and eyes in tones of amber and umber.

△ A neutral base coat enables you to pick out the details in any colours you choose, from pale blues and greys to strong primary colours as on the chairs above. For an opulent effect, in imitation of some of the Far Eastern styles, you could paint the bamboo black or lacquer red with gold details, or in tones of turquoise or jade with contrasting details.

Tortoiseshelling

*For thousands of years the beautiful translucent shell
of the hawksbill sea turtle provided a rich adornment — for a
price. Now, despite the trade ban on 'tortoiseshell', you can still
capture its unique attraction by the careful application
of straightforward painting techniques.*

Like many fantasy paint techniques, tortoiseshelling was developed to provide an inexpensive substitute for a much sought after commodity. Real tortoiseshell has always been a rare and precious adornment — even before the current concern for animal welfare.

In 1973 the hawksbill sea turtle — source of the much coveted 'tortoiseshell' — was declared an endangered species and a world trade ban was agreed.

However, the attraction of the shell, with its distinctive brown and black markings, and beige, tawny and blond shades — even reds — remains unforgettable.

The scarcity of the raw material has tended to limit its use to smaller items such as on hair brushes, picture frames and trays, or for use as inlay on furniture.

The fake paint method does not

have this limitation but is nevertheless best used on small objects where it produces the quickest and most authentic results. The finish is time consuming — worth considering before embarking on a major project such as a table top.

Tortoiseshelling can also be worked in bright colour combinations — blue and green for example — or can be combined with a plain marble or simulated ivory finish, but don't go over the top.

▽ An Antwerp tortoiseshell and ebony veneered cabinet on a stand dating from the third quarter of the 17th Century. A plain cabinet at home could be 'dressed' with the tortoiseshell look.

The look of tortoiseshell
It is a good idea to keep a piece of real tortoiseshell or a picture of it by you as you work, but try to capture the essence of tortoiseshell rather than aim for a photographic representation of the natural markings which may look laboured.

The markings are created by applying tinted glaze in oval-shaped patches on to a paler background. The pattern should run diagonally across the work — preferably a flat or slightly curved surface — with bands of colour diverging slightly. Work in a diagonal direction when building up the pattern. Blend in the glaze at the edges to imitate the graduations in colour which occur in real tortoiseshell. The darkest tone should be at the centre of the markings, fading to rich chestnut and golden brown at the edges.

Materials and equipment
Paints
Remember you will not need huge pots of paint if you are working on small items.

Base coat Use two coats of an oil-based paint with an eggshell or similar soft sheen finish. Gloss paint is too shiny for tortoiseshelling. The colours used depend on the final colouring you want to achieve; the base coat is usually quite a strong chrome or acid yellow. Bare wood needs sealing first with a primer/undercoat product.

Top coat For a realistic tortoiseshell effect, make the first layer of glaze from 70 per cent scumble, 20 per cent white spirit and 10 per cent artists' oil in raw sienna. The markings are made by tinting the glaze with artists' oils in progressively darker shades of burnt umber and black.

Varnish
Clear polyurethane varnish is essential to protect the finish. Decorative items need only two coats of varnish but anything subject to wear (such as a table or tray) should be given three coats. Choose a mid sheen varnish for a natural look and add a trace of white gloss to prevent yellowing. Varnish dries quickly so it is essential to work fast. For this reason, don't work on too large an area at once. If you intend to cover a large area, work in alternate panels, leaving each to dry before tackling the next.

Brushes
For the best results use specialist brushes. You need an ordinary paint brush for applying the base coat, an artists' 'fitch' for the glaze, a softening brush for blending and a small stencil brush for spattering. A piece of lint free cloth is also needed for softening the surface of the glaze to give a more natural-looking finished result.

Preparing the surface

Strip the piece clean of any polish using white spirit and wire wool followed by detergent solution. Metal or wood items must be sanded down (wood should be sanded along the grain). Treat bare wood with a coat of primer/undercoat. For metal, use an appropriate primer followed by undercoat.

1 Apply two coats of buff colour eggshell paint, sanding lightly with dampened silicon carbide paper between each coat, then wiping clean to give a fine finish. Work diagonally throughout.

2 Apply a coat of glaze with the fitch, working back and forth to create a dragged effect.

3 Still working diagonally, soften the lines by dabbing the glaze with a lint free cloth.

4 To create the characteristic tortoiseshell markings, add more raw sienna to the glaze to darken it and apply with the fitch in oval-shaped patches about 5-7 cm long. Keep the outline random, overlapping it from time to time.

5 Add burnt umber to the mix to darken it again and make further marks inside the patches. Then add more burnt umber and a touch of black for the darkest markings and apply in the centre of the previous burnt umber marks.

6 Blur the outlines with a softening brush, working the colours in well so that they merge into each other. Finish by blending away any remaining hard outlines with a random movement of the brush. If the glaze is still wet you can repeat this process to give an even more realistic effect.

7 Spatter tiny dots of the darkest glaze over the surface using a small stencil brush. Dip no more than one third of the bristle length into the paint. Tap the base of the handle against a straight edge held over the work and aim to create a fine shower of paint.

8 If you want to break up the pattern you can ciss the surface while it is still wet, giving an antique effect. Load an artists' brush with white spirit and tap it against a stick held over the surface of the work. It takes a few seconds for the effect to become noticeable. Tap lightly and leave for half a minute.

9 Allow the glaze to dry and then apply polyurethane varnish for protection. Rub this down with fine glass paper and clean between coats. Several coats of varnish create a deep, protective sheen, enhancing the effect.

△ *In this traditional style reception room the decor has been given the tortoiseshelling treatment, with the painting technique applied to the door frames and the cornice.*

Colours

Natural tortoiseshell has a beauty of its own but the design also lends itself to other deep, rich colours. Try blending green and dark blue on a sea coloured background, or combine ruby red with dark brown for a sophisticated effect.

For a successful finish, simply remember to keep to related colours, choosing a pale tone for the background and building up the markings with increasingly saturated shades so that the darkest shade is in the centre. The darkest shade is also used for the drops, which are spattered lightly over the surface for a naturalistic effect.

△ *Here are three entirely different looks created by using the same 'tortoiseshelling' techniques. The bottom two examples use different colour combinations from the traditional browns.*

Porphyry

Although porphyry rock is neither rare nor expensive, it is an easy and popular stone to recreate successfully using paints. Its natural grainy appearance is imitated by spattering varying tones of a chosen colour over a solid base colour.

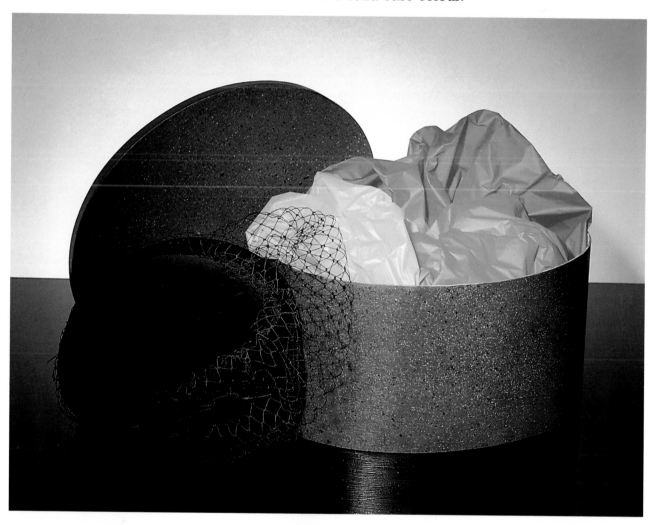

What is porphyry?

Porphyry is an igneous rock with a grainy appearance. Highly polished, and hard and cool to the touch, it is similar to marble, except that it has few or no veins. Although it is usually reddish purple, porphyry does occur in a range of other colours including green or violet; reddish orange; and brown, veined with quartz and speckled with pink, red and green. Some types of porphyry also contain tiny speckles of iron (fool's gold).

Real porphyry is used mainly to make small objects, such as table and desk tops, decorative inlays and ornamental bases for stands. For an impressive paint effect, try copying the appearance of this stone to decorate boxes, plain lamp bases and other small items of furniture.

Creating the effect

The best results are achieved by imitating the natural colours of real porphyry. A porphyry finish is created by spattering the base colour with three or more tones of the same colours.

The spattering should be dense enough to cover most of the base colour. The spatter effect can be made finer or coarser by tapping closer and farther away from the surface; alternatively, for larger spatters, thin the paint mixture with white spirit. Glaze is used for the base colour but it should not be added to the spatter mixture, as it will produce a lumpy, uneven finish.

Materials and equipment

Artists' oil colours in three toning shades, a transparent glaze and white spirit are needed for painting this finish, plus a range of good quality brushes and a mutton cloth.

You will need
◇ Artists' oils: alizarin crimson, burnt sienna, burnt umber and titanium white
◇ Transparent oil glaze
◇ White spirit (to thin the glaze slightly)
◇ Large fitch and small fitch
◇ Mutton cloth
◇ Badger hair softening brush
◇ Gloss varnish
◇ Paint tray

Method

1 If necessary, prepare the surface by sanding any rough areas with abrasive paper and then priming. Wear rubber gloves to protect your hands.

2 Make a deep, reddish purple coloured glaze by mixing the ingredients together in the following proportions: 45 per cent alizarin crimson; 30 per cent burnt sienna; 10 per cent burnt umber; 10 per cent glaze and 5 per cent white spirit. Using the large fitch, apply it thinly and evenly to the surface; try to produce varying tones of colour.

3 Bunch the mutton cloth into a pad in your hand and gently pat the glazed surface to remove any brush strokes and surplus paint.

4 To remove any remaining marks, lightly touch over the surface with the softening brush, taking care not to add any more brush marks.

5 Mix the artists' oils separately with a little white spirit to make red, dusky pink and red-brown colour (if necessary, add a little titanium white).

6 Dip the small fitch in one of the mixtures and then wipe it against the side of the paint tray to test the consistency of the paint. For spattering, the paint should be quite runny.

7 To spatter the paint finely, hold the fitch in one hand and drag the index finger of the other hand through the bristle tips – remember that the thicker the mixture is, the smaller the spatters will be. If you want bigger blobs, thin the mixture first with white spirit.

8 Repeat the spattering technique with the other two colours.

9 Leave to dry overnight. Then, for a polished finish, cover with two coats of gloss varnish.

The art of stencilling

*In a world dominated by mass-produced designs
and patterns, the simple technique of painting colour through a
decorative cut-out shape enables you to create
your own beautiful designs and colour schemes, and to experiment
and to express yourself in your own home.*

Stencilling is infinitely versatile. It can be used to make patterns or to create large, bold effects; it can produce a single motif or a border design; and it can be used to decorate walls, furniture and lampshades. It is the perfect way to produce tailor-made and co-ordinated decorations that are also individual.

The materials and techniques for stencilling on surfaces such as plaster, paint, wood and metal are described on the following pages. You can create interesting effects on textures such as basketwork and cane furniture. Many different weights and finishes of fabric can also be successfully stencilled, from plain closely woven cottons to textured cloths and sheers. Stencilling on fabric is covered on pages 77-82.

Surfaces should be clean, sound and preferably smooth. If you wish to stencil on to natural wood, for example, floors or furniture, you can work directly on to the surface. Try a small area to see if the colour 'bleeds' along the grain. If it does, seal it first with a coat of clear matt varnish. It is essential to remove any old varnish or polish before starting (the new paint will not adhere permanently to a glossy varnish or a waxy surface).

Materials and equipment
Paints
Whichever type of paint you use, you will need only a small amount; a small tube or pot should be sufficient.

Water-based paints are fast-drying, enabling you to work quickly without smudging the work.

Emulsion paints come in a limited colour range, but can be tinted with acrylic paints.

Artist's acrylic paints come in a wide range of colours and can also be mixed together to create the exact shade you want. They are stocked by most art shops.

Oil-based paints Matt eggshell paint is durable and effective but takes longer to dry than a water-based paint.

Other paints Water- and oil-based stencil crayons are available from specialist shops. When using oil-based crayons, rub on to an uncut area of the stencil and then use this as a 'palette' for charging the brush with paint. Metallic powders, spray paints and wood stains can also be used.

Varnish Surfaces subject to heavy wear will need sealing. Use a clear matt or gloss polyurethane varnish and apply two to four days after stencilling so that the paint has had time to dry out thoroughly.

△ Before stencilling, the knob on this wooden drawer was taken off and the old paint removed. The wood was sealed with matt varnish. After stencilling, further coats of varnish were applied to the stencilled re-assembled drawer for a durable finish.

Stencils
Ready-made stencils are available in a whole range of designs from large DIY stores, some art and craft shops and specialist suppliers (often by mail order). You can buy stencils ready-cut or with the areas marked out for you to cut out.

Most stencils are made from waxed manila card or acetate sheet. Some stencils have a different sheet for each colour and each one must be accurately positioned. Others have the whole design on one sheet if you are working with more than one colour, you must block out, or mask, one area with tape while working on another.

Acetate is transparent, so you can see the other colours through it and position the stencil more accurately. Acetate does, however, have a tendency to curl.

Manila is the traditional stencilling material. It is stable to work with, but not so easy for a beginner as you cannot tell if it is lined up perfectly until you've finished applying the colour.

Brushes
Stencil brushes are round with short stiff bristles which have been cut square at the end to give a soft, stippled effect. They are available in a variety of sizes. Ideally, you should buy a brush for each colour and match the size of brush to the scale of the design.

It is important to clean the brushes whenever you finish working. Clean brushes in warm soapy water when using water-based paints, and white spirit if using oil-based paint. To ensure that the bristles keep a good shape when drying, use an elastic band to hold them together. Never leave brushes bristles-down in water or white spirit as this ruins their shape.

Sponges
You can use a natural or synthetic sponge to apply paint through the stencil. Cut the sponge into small pieces and use them to dab on the colour. This gives a pleasant textured look to the final design and is particularly effective over large areas of plain colour.

Manila stencil

Acetate stencil

Paint tray

Paint

Masking tape

Brushes

Brass stencil

Natural sponge

Stencilling a single-coloured motif

1 Pour some paint into a saucer. If necessary dilute it with a little water (water-based paint) or white spirit (oil-based paint). The consistency of the paint should be creamy — if it is too thin it will run and seep under the edge of the stencil.

2 Position the stencil and fix it in place with masking tape. Dip the brush into the paint and remove any excess on scrap paper.

3 Using one hand to press the stencil firmly against the surface, dab paint on to the stencil until the cut-out areas are filled.

4 Leave the paint to dry. Remove the tape and lift off the stencil. Don't slide the stencil or you'll smudge the work. Clean off the stencil when you've finished with a soft rag dipped in soapy water (for water-based paints) or white spirit (for oil-based paints). Store stencils flat when dry.

△ *A delicate green leaf design decorates this panelled door. The moulding is picked out in a lighter tone of the same colour. Doors lend themselves to stencilling with both borders and single motifs. Panels within doors are a natural defined space for decoration with coloured motifs.*

TIP COLOUR SHADING

Subtle colouring is more attractive for most subjects than solid areas of colour and adds to the hand-done appeal. Use the brush fairly dry so that it makes a stippled mark rather than a solid blob. To create interest and subtle shading on single colour areas, build up the colour in certain areas. A similar effect can be achieved with a sponge.

Stencilling a multi-coloured motif

Using a single stencil

If the whole design is contained on a single stencil, you can complete the painting without removing the stencil. Simply mask off all but the area you are working on each time using small pieces of paper or card and masking tape.

Using a series of stencils

If there is a separate stencil for each colour, position and paint your first stencil and let it dry. Now plan the position of the next stencil.

Acetate stencils are transparent so you can see the area already painted through the stencil and can therefore position the second and subsequent stencils accordingly.

Manila card stencils obscure painted areas so mark the position of the corners of the first stencil with a light pencil before removing it — these are known as registration marks. Match up the corners of subsequent stencils with these marks.

Stencilling borders

*Now that you have mastered the basics of stencilling
and experimented with individual motifs, why not try your hand
at border designs? These can be used to enhance
a room with few architectural details, or as a way of
emphasizing existing features.*

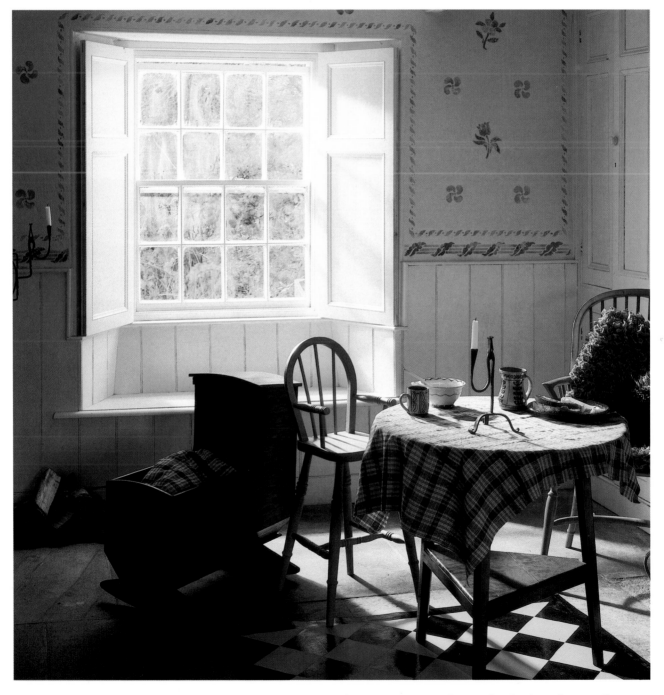

Border stencils can be used in many ways to enhance
features and co-ordinate a look. There are numerous
designs available to suit every taste and style —
modern, traditional, folk or classical motifs abound.

△ *A delicate, continuous border in soft, muted
colours has been used to create patterned 'panels' and
accentuate the elegant window.*

Planning the design

Before you can begin stencilling you need to work out and mark the position of each motif. This is particularly important with continuous, architectural borders or for smaller borders. For freer designs or where motifs are spaced out along a wall, it is not so critical.

When stencilling on walls, bear in mind that they are rarely absolutely straight and the corners are hardly ever at true right angles. This means that you cannot use the walls as an accurate guide and, even with the most careful planning, you often need to make final adjustments by eye.

Positioning the border

1 Marking the vertical Use a plumb line to find the true vertical and mark with chalk; only draw in the area to be stencilled. The chalk can be rubbed out when you have finished stencilling.

2 Marking the horizontal Using a set square, mark a horizontal line at right angles to the vertical one, and level with the top or bottom of your stencil. Position the stencil on this line.

Non-continuous border

This is a repeated single motif spaced evenly around a room. Take each wall separately and calculate how many times the stencil will fit into the space - the spacing between the motifs should be equal. On plain walls, work outwards from the centre of each wall. If there is a feature (a chimney breast) placed off-centre, feature and walls either side are treated separately and the first motif centred each time.

Continuous border

1 Some patterns are designed to be a continuous band. Keeping the border level (even if your surface is not), calculate how many times the stencil fits into the space with each motif touching — you will probably have to cheat with the last motif so start in a corner or somewhere unobtrusive.

2 To turn a corner, calculate where on the stencil the angle will occur. Place a metal ruler along this line and score it with the back of a scalpel or craft knife. For an inward angle score the back of the stencil; for an outward one, score the front. Bend the stencil over the ruler to make a smooth fold.

Mitring a corner

1 Mark the horizontal line as before. Using a set square, draw a line at an angle of 45° to cross it. Place masking tape along the line.

2 Stencil along the horizontal line, taking the paint over the edge of the tape. Remove tape and leave the motif until thoroughly dry.

3 Reposition the tape along the other side of diagonal line; over the completed work. Repeat as before. When dry, rub out the line.

Note: Do not worry too much about finding the perfect area of the stencil for the mitre.

Whether stencilling a panel, around a door or window, it is almost inevitable that not all the mitres will be at an ideal part of the design. You will, in fact, find that once the design is completed, any discrepancy is hardly noticeable.

Toy box

You will need
◇ Cardboard box
◇ Stencil brush or sponge
◇ Prepared stencil
◇ Emulsion paint for base
◇ Acrylic, stencil or emulsion
  paints for the design
◇ Masking tape

Paint the box with emulsion and leave to dry. Fix the stencil in position with masking tape. Cover the areas not being stencilled and apply the first colour. Allow to dry and repeat with subsequent colours. For added protection coat the finished box with varnish.

△ *A plain cardboard box is transformed into a cheerful children's toy box using our geometric stencil design.*

Tracing stencils from printed designs

Stencil designs must be transferred on to a stencil sheet before cutting. The easiest way is to trace the design on to transparent acetate. With masking tape, secure the acetate in position over the design and trace along the outline of the pattern. To ensure a flowing, continuous line, hold the pen in a relaxed way. Draw straight lines with a ruler.

Cutting out the stencil

With masking tape, stick the stencil firmly to a cutting board or mat. Using a scalpel or craft knife, cut along the outline. A sure, continuous line is best, so be confident. If you are tentative, the line will look jerky and show on the stencilled design. For long, curved lines, it is easier to move the board around as you work, rather than the blade.

BORDERS

These attractive border patterns can be used on a wall, door, piece of furniture or any other suitable item. Choice of colours depends on the room and the background colour of the design. You can use a single colour for simplicity, or choose a range of several contrasting colours. Alternatively, you might decide on a two-tone effect worked in a light and dark version of the same colour. Pale colours can look effective on a dark background; dark colours are often enhanced by a lighter background. The finished effect depends entirely on your choice of colours, so it is worth giving these some thought and even trying out a few different colour combinations on pieces of scrap paper before you begin stencilling.

◁ An elegant geometric border stencil has been chosen to compliment the proportions of this hallway. The depth of the cornice stencil visually reduces the ceiling height and a narrower stencil using part of the same motif links the dado rail to the cornice.

▽ An informal continous vine border has been placed deliberately to frame this dining area. Note how some of the details — grapes, figs and fig leaves — have been used individually to give extra dimensions to the border.

Spray stencilling

*Car aerosol paints are excellent for all forms of
stencilling and they can be used very successfully on all types
of surfaces, from walls and floors to furniture and
fabric. Here, spray paints and floral stencils have been used to
decorate fabric for curtains and a chair cover.*

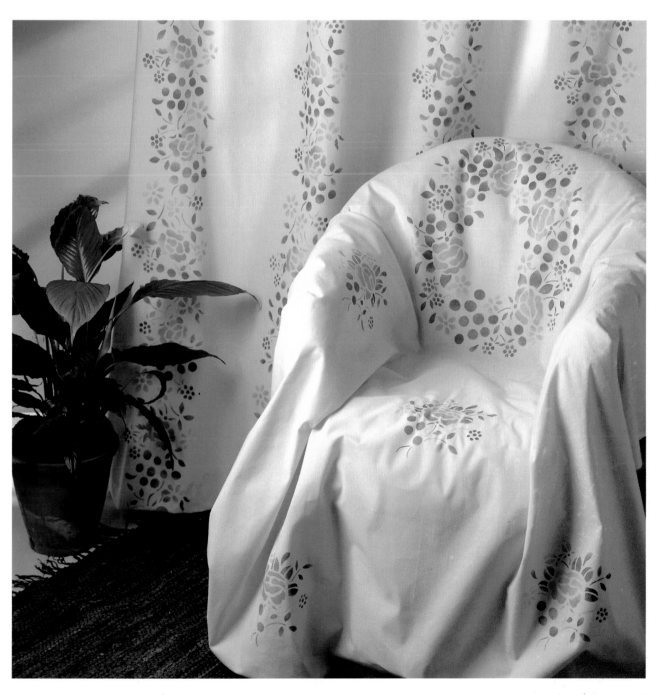

One of the joys of stencilling is allowing the colours to overlap, to create a wonderfully shaded and muted effect. Aerosol paints are ideal for achieving these mellow effects: they can be applied lightly and, as they dry quickly, thin veils of colour can be easily blended.

△ Use the floral stencils, shown overleaf, to transform plain calico into charming, delicately-shaded furnishings to brighten a room.

Stencilled fabric

When using aerosol paints, it is important to remember to use the paint very thinly, building up the colours gradually. Since the paint dries quickly there is no need to wait before adding the next colour. Do not worry about colour variations in the finished items, as this will add to the overall effect. When aerosols are used correctly, a subtle· overlapping of colour will enhance the final effect. If you want the colours to be more defined, cut separate masks for each colour.

You will need
◇ Car aerosol paint: we used dark green, light blue, dark blue, pale yellow and cherry red
◇ Stencil acetate
◇ Fabric: we used unbleached calico
◇ Kitchen towel
◇ Masking tape

Method

1 Place the fabric on to a clean, flat surface. Spray back of stencil with spray adhesive. Leave for a moment to become tacky to the touch; then position it on to the fabric and press down firmly, making sure that no gaps are left between the stencil and the fabric for the paint to seep underneath.

2 Carefully mask round the stencil with kitchen towel and masking tape to protect the surrounding fabric from the spray paint.

3 Starting with the green aerosol paint, lightly spray the leaves and foliage in the design, holding a piece of card in your other hand to help direct the spray. Add touches of yellow and cherry red — leaves are seldom just green and adding other colours gives a natural, mellow look.

PATTERN EXTRA

4 Spray the roses and daisies with pale yellow paint. To make the peach coloured roses, spray a little cherry red on to the outer petals. To shade the colour in this way hold your piece of card round the edge of the rose to actually aim the paint at the base of the card. In this way a little of the paint will be deflected on to the rose petals.

5 To shade the grapes, use some pale blue spray, followed by less of the dark blue; for luscious looking grapes add a little cherry red at outer edges. For brambles, use dark blue paint with a touch of cherry. During this, the daisies will have caught a little of each colour and will blend in well.

6 Periodically lift a corner of the stencil to inspect your progress — the image will look stronger when the stencil is lifted. Once satisfied with the effect, remove the stencil. Re-apply adhesive and stencil the next section.

Border stencil

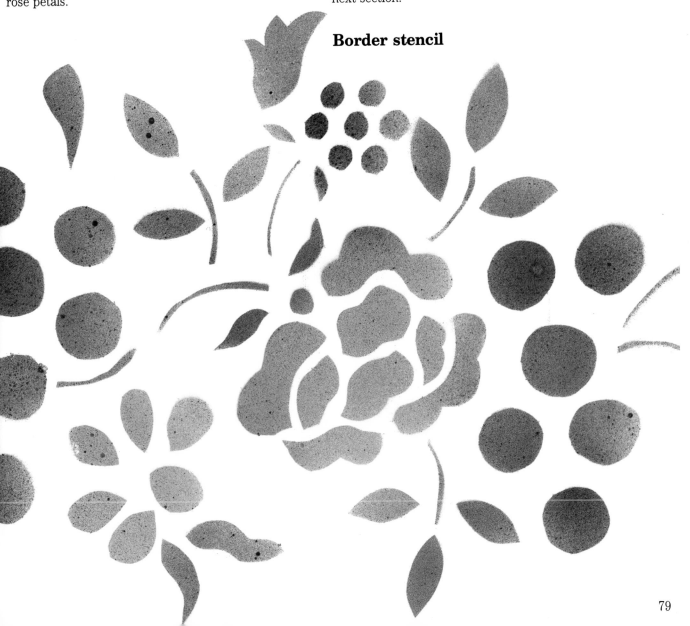

Circular stencil

◁ △ *This garland design was adapted from the border stencil on the previous page. To use the circular stencil, trace the pattern on to acetate, repeating some of the motifs to make a complete circle.*

▷ *Use this individual motif to decorate small items or scatter it around a larger design.*

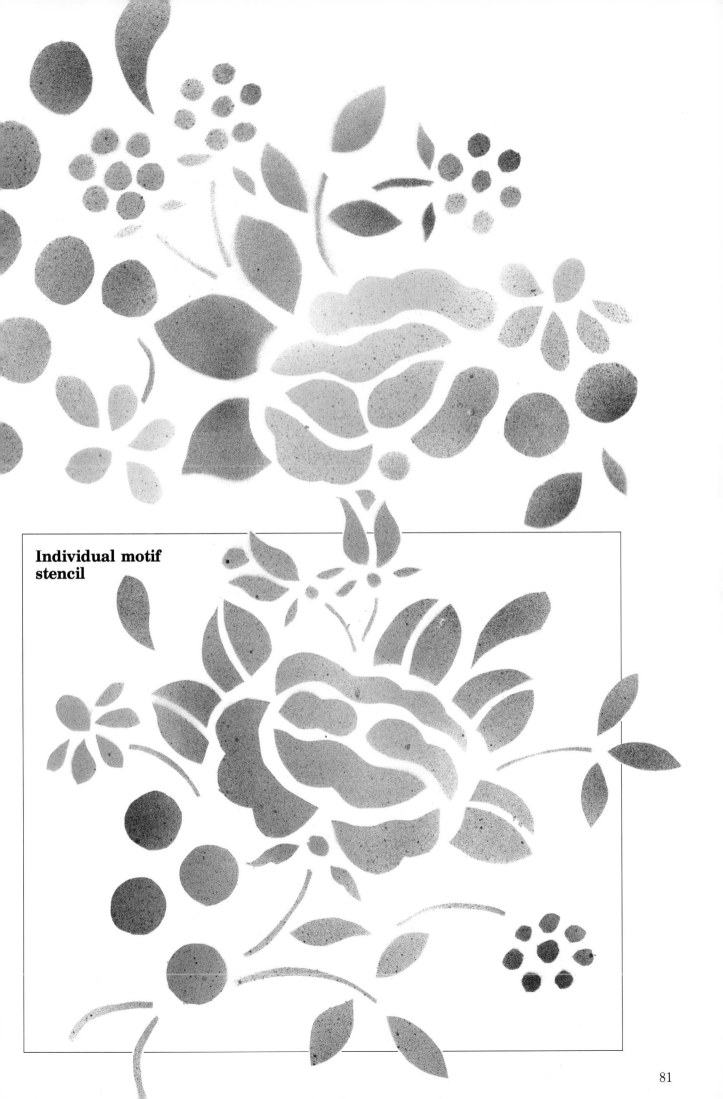

**Individual motif
stencil**

Using aerosol paints

Aerosol paints come in a vast range of colours, though only a few cans are needed to create a wide spectrum of shades. The paint is acrylic-based and therefore dries almost instantly, enabling you to work more quickly. However, it is important to apply the paint evenly and very sparingly, otherwise unattractive, hard blocks of colour could be formed. This is easy to judge: if the surface looks wet, too much paint is being used.

To use the paint, hold the can about 8in (20cm) from the surface and, using a gentle pumping action, spray in short bursts to give a thin layer of colour. Hold a piece of card in your other hand to help direct the spray and protect the rest of the stencil.

Before you start, perfect your technique by practising on paper or spare scraps of fabric. This will enable you to see how the colours are going to work together. With practise, you will soon master the technique and gain confidence.

Suitable fabrics

All kinds of fabric can be stencilled, but always experiment first to ensure that you achieve the desired result. Natural fabrics are particularly nice to use as they absorb the paint well to produce lovely, soft colours that highlight the shaded areas.

Fabric that has been stencilled with car aerosol paint must either be dry-cleaned or carefully hand washed in warm water and mild detergent. Do not wash the stencilled fabric in a washing machine as this will cause the colours to fade.

Cutting stencils in masks

With more complex stencils it is worthwhile cutting several stencils, or masks, for the various colours. This will enable you to work more quickly as there is no need to protect the different areas of the stencil from the individual colours being used. However, it is still important to shade the colours carefully to allow for some overlap of colour, otherwise the result may appear too slick and rigid.

To repeat the stencil for each different colour, lay the master stencil on a sheet of stencil film and use the spray paint to stencil a copy of the film. Repeat this to make as many masks as required, keeping each mask to one colour of the pattern and only cutting out the motifs needing those colours. Make sure that you

△ *When using aerosols, always wear a mask and work in a well-ventilated room. Protect areas not to be painted with paper and use card to angle the spray.*

have register marks on each stencil, to enable you to position each one accurately. Always work in the same sequence and lift off each mask as it is completed before positioning the next one.

Using the stencils

As with other stencilling methods, it is essential to stick the stencil firmly to the surface being painted: for the best results use a spray adhesive that enables you to reposition the stencil. Using an adhesive helps to prevent paint seeping under the stencil which will spoil the clean edge of the design.

Once the stencil is in position, surround it with kitchen paper, attached with masking tape. This will protect other areas from the drift of spray.

Design ideas

These informal, rather random floral designs are very adaptable and easy for the novice to use, as opposed to geometric patterns which require very careful positioning. The border design illustrated here can be used vertically or horizontally and just butted up where it turns a corner.

To transform a small room, use the border panel to decorate the walls at dado or cornice level. It would also make handsome tie-backs, which could be attached to curtains made from darker fabric which is less suitable to stencil.

The oval garland, used on the chair cover, would also look attractive stencilled on top of a chest of drawers or a small table. You could then use the border design across the drawer fronts and parts of the garland to make swags to decorate the sides.

Try combining both designs to transform large, plain curtains. Work a repeat pattern, with the oval garland placed between the stripes of the border design, across the width of the fabric.

The little posy design could be dotted about on walls inside the stencilled border to give a cottagey effect. Alternatively, use it inside a cupboard door or under the lid of a chest to give an unexpected, pleasing feature when the lid is opened.

Block printing

*Printing is simply the transfer of inks or dyes by
means of pressure. Block printing is the simplest form of
this craft and its great advantage is that it
can be used to produce very effective results at home — without
the need to buy any expensive equipment.*

Block printing

This simple and direct printing technique can be used on almost any surface. It is an ideal way to brighten up a plain wall or decorate a large piece of furniture, even to print a length of fabric.

Block printing has survived as an art form for over 2000 years, and part of the reason for this lies in its versatility. A variety of materials can be used to make the printing block ranging from wood and lino to string and crumpled paper. Another advantage of block printing is that you don't have to learn how to register a print — pleasing and dramatic effects can be created by using just one colour. Don't be too ambitious at first, try printing a small area using a simple repeat pattern, before commiting yourself to the whole room or a pair of curtains or a bedspread.

Handprinting is always irregular, so don't worry if each printed motif looks different. These variations will add to the final effect. If, however, the surface you are printing on is uneven, a sponge block is by far the best because it is flexible enough to print over most uneven surfaces.

△ *The range of materials that can be used as the printing block is limited only by your imagination. Try experimenting with pasta shapes, pieces of string and crumpled tissue paper mounted on a block to create a variety of interesting textured prints.*

Tools and equipment

The basic materials required for block printing are very simple. Many of the items, such as a sharp blade or craft knife, glue and a paintbrush, you may well already have. You will also need:

Paint

You can use household emulsion, artists' acrylics or children's PVA paints. The latter are particularly good because they are relatively inexpensive and come in a range of bright colours. Acrylic dries quickly, and is therefore only suitable for small areas.

Whichever paint you use, it should not be too runny — the consistency of thick cream is about right. All the paints are water based which makes cleaning up easy. For printing on fabric, use special fabric colours with an appropriate thickener and fix colours in place by ironing.

Blocks

Printing blocks can be made by either carving out a shape from the block or by mounting a textured surface on to the block to form a relief motif. One of the simplest forms of block printing is potato printing — a method often used to introduce the craft to children, but the technique can be easily adapted and upgraded to suit the most sophisticated tastes.

Traditionally wood, lino or heavy cardboard have been used to make blocks but other mediums can be used. Polystyrene and simple household sponges both make effective blocks with the added advantage that they are easy to carve.

The following pages demonstrate how to make block prints using an ordinary household sponge as the printing block.

Using a roller

Using a roller ensures that the paint is applied evenly to the relief surface. This is important as it avoids some parts of the printed design being very faint in appearance while others look clogged. Although slight variations in the density of the paint are part of the charm of block printing, it is worth taking some care to avoid the overall effect being too messy.

Printing surfaces

It is possible to print on most surfaces including fabric and wood, wool and paper.

Sponge printing

If you are working with single motif designs shaped from a sponge, or a block of sponge on a relatively small area, then mounting on wood is not necessary. This is the simplest method of block printing.

1 Draw the outline of your design with felt tip pen or pencil on to a synthetic sponge (a close-grained sponge gives a dense print, a coarser sponge produces a more textured effect). Use a sharp scalpel or craft knife to neatly cut away all the areas that you do not want to print.

2 Here the background area is cut away to produce a raised petal shape suitable for a random scattered design. A single motif can also be cut from the flat side of a halved potato.

3 To print, pour the colour into a shallow container and dip in the sponge, cut side down. Apply the block firmly to the surface to be painted, taking care not to smudge the design. One colour application should last for several prints.

4 To obtain a sharp edge to your design, stick a length of masking tape firmly to the surface before applying the paint. Take the printed colour up to and over the tape. When the colour is dry, remove the tape to reveal the straight edge.

Mounting a sponge block

To make sponge block last longer it can be mounted onto a thin piece of wood or heavy cardboard. Shape the sponge first, then glue it to the wood using a waterproof glue like PVA adhesive. The block will be easier to use if it has a handle on the back. This will also prevent you covering your hands with paint too. An old cupboard handle, mounted onto the back of the block, makes an ideal handle. You could also use a smaller square of wood, glued in place on the back, as a handle.

▷ *Trace your design onto a sponge with a felt tip pen and use a sharp knife to cut away the areas you do not wish to print.*

△ *Mount the sponge block on to a flat piece of wood for easy handling. Here we have used a piece of wood with a wooden cupboard knob screwed to the back.*

△ *The paint can also be applied with a paintbrush, although a roller will give a more even paint coverage. Apply the paint evenly to the relief surface. Make sure the paint you are using isn't too runny.*

▽ *A simple repeat pattern using just one colour can produce very effective results. The sponge block gives a wonderfully textured print, that works well applied to a slightly textured surface like this wall.*

Painting on furniture

*Transform tatty furniture and shabby household
objects into original works of art by painting them with bold
geometric patterns and motifs. You don't need to be
an expert artist to achieve pleasing results that will liven
up your home.*

Doors, chairs, cupboards, in fact any item in the home, can begin to look rather 'tired' with age and detract from the overall appearance of a room. Instead of replacing items or simply covering them with a coat of paint, why not create a bright and unusual scheme by painting them with orignal designs or motifs.

Freehand designs have a charm and appeal all of their own, which is far less structured than other decorative techniques like stencilling.

Don't worry if you cannot draw as you can still produce stunning results. Use everyday objects as templates for bold geometric designs or try copying the designs in books or even wallpaper designs if they are reasonably simple.

Materials and equipment

Many items such as glasspaper, rags, paper, pencil and scissors, you may already have at home. However, you will need to purchase brushes, varnish and paints to suit the surface to be painted.

Paints

The paint you choose will depend on the surface you are decorating.

Emulsion and acrylic paints These are used when painting on wood. Emulsion is inexpensive and ideal for covering large areas such as doors, wall panels and pieces of furniture. Artists' acrylics are more costly but come in a wide range of vibrant colours and are extremely tough and durable. It is possible to combine emulsion and acrylic paints. For example, it is often a good idea to paint large, background areas with emulsion, then paint the smaller motifs in bright acrylics. Alternatively, you can mix the two paints together as they are both water-based. Emulsion takes several hours to dry, whereas acrylic dries in a few minutes.

Ceramic paints When decorating tiles and other glazed surfaces use special ceramic paints. These are available from good art and craft shops. As these paints are not water-based, you must also buy a suitable diluter.

Metal paints Special paints and enamels are available for painting metal. Follow the manufacturer's instructions for diluter, preparation and drying time.

Varnishes

A coat of clear matt or gloss varnish protects the finished painted surface and will enhance the colours. In rooms likely to get splashed by water — bathrooms and kitchens — painted surfaces benefit from two or three coats of varnish. Table tops and other surfaces subject to wear and tear should also be protected with several coats of varnish.

Brushes

Choose a brush in a size that suits the area you wish to paint. Use decorating brushes to paint large areas. For small areas and intricate patterns use artists' brushes. Wash all brushes immediately after use. This is very important when using quick-drying acrylics because if this paint is allowed to dry on the bristles, the brushes will no longer be usable.

Preparation

Surfaces must be smooth and free from dirt and grease. Old paintwork should be washed thoroughly and rubbed down with glasspaper to remove loose particles of paint and roughen the surface — this enables the new paint to adhere to the old. Always prime new wood before applying a basecoat.

If there are any cracks or flaws in the surface, fill them with a proprietary filler, following the manufacturer's instructions. Then rub down with glasspaper before painting the basecoat.

Planning designs

Bold patterns and loosely painted motifs, such as those featured in this bathroom, are effective and easy to do. However, the success of this seemingly casual effect depends on careful planning. Both your design and colour scheme must be carefully thought out before you start painting.

Plan your design on paper first, keeping it as simple as possible. Try basing the design on geometric shapes, such as ovals and circles, which can be adapted to create a wide variety of interesting shapes and designs.

Same-size designs

If you are painting a fairly small area, such as a chair seat, you can make a pencil drawing of your design on a piece of paper that is the same size as the chair seat.

To transfer the design to the seat, scribble over the back of the paper with a soft pencil, then position the paper on the chair, with the original design face up. Trace firmly over the original lines of the pattern — only draw the main outlines of the design as the details can be painted in later. Alternatively, transfer the design by drawing a grid over it and copying it, square by square, on to a similar grid drawn directly on to the chair seat.

Enlarging designs

If you are painting a large area, such as the side of a bath, it may be impractical to make a drawing of the same size. In this case, make a smaller drawing, in proportion to the area to be painted, and mark a grid over the top. To transfer the design, mark up the surface to be painted with the same number of squares but proportionately larger, then copy the design square by square on to the surface.

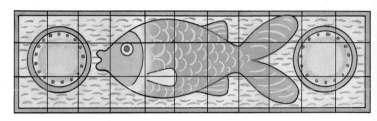

Using templates

When painting simple or repeated designs, you can save time by making a template. Cut your chosen shapes out of paper or cardboard and then draw around them on to the surface you are painting. Alternatively, create circles, ovals and squares by drawing round household objects such as dishes, plates and boxes.

△ *To make this continuous curved motif, first draw five circles using a template, then adapt them as shown here.*

△ *Simple designs are often the most effective of all. This floral design is built up from geometric shapes — a circle for the flower motif and curves for the leaves. Use plates as the templates.*

Freehand designs

Many designs can be painted directly on to your surface without the use of a template. However, it is still advisable to make a rough sketch first so that you are clear about the design before you begin.

If there are a lot of repeated shapes in the design it is a good idea to combine the use of templates with more original freehand images.

Choosing colours

Choice of colour is very personal, however, whatever shades you choose to use, it is essential to plan the scheme carefully. Try experimenting on a piece of paper with different colour combinations using other tones in the room as a base. If you wish to totally transform a room, make sure that you create a harmonious scene by creating a visual colour link between the different items.

DESIGN IDEAS

▷ *A sideboard is given a new lease of life with a floral pattern to complement the existing decor.*

◁ *'Frame' a fireplace with your own picture painted on to surrounding tiles with ceramic paints. This hearth is a good example of breaking free from traditional fireplace colours and motifs.*

▽ *An aspect of a plain kitchen — the door — is used to advantage here for interest and warmth. One strutting grey chicken, artfully topped with red, brings life and humour to the room.*

Painting frames

*Decoratively painted frames give a new lease of
life to the prints and paintings they contain. A hand-painted
frame, specially designed to set off a favourite
picture, photograph or mirror, gives an enchanting finishing
touch to the decoration of a room.*

Turn prints, postcards, or even tear sheets from magazines, into unusual pictures for your walls by mounting them in customized frames. Inexpensive wooden, metal and plastic frames can all be given the designer touch. All it takes is for you to paint them imaginatively, so that they complement and bring

to life the picture they hold.

Break all the rules of framing, which preach that the frame should play second fiddle to the picture, by making it part of the picture. This can be used effectively for inexpensive postcards or prints, that need an individual touch to loose their mass-produced look.

△ *The design of this bright and cheerful painted frame has been inspired by the picture it holds. The colours and motifs of the abstract design were taken from the patterned tablecloth. They were then drawn on to the primed frame in pencil and painted, using bold primary colours.*

◁ *The inspiration for the garden motif on this frame came from the leaves and flowers depicted in the print. These shapes were used as design ideas, but were simplified to form a repeat pattern of leaves around the frame. Soft pastel shades were used to complement the colour of the vase and flowers.*

Design ideas

When decorating the frame, be inspired by the print you have chosen. For the easiest approach, pick out two colours in the print and paint simple motifs or abstract patterns. Stripes of repeated stencilled motifs, or dashes of colour, work well. If the picture depicts a rural scene, use leaves and flowers as design ideas, but simplify them. For instance, decide on a shape and use this as a repeated pattern. The more adventurous may like to try recreating a section of the picture around the frame.

Colours

The joy of designing and painting your own frame comes from the satisfaction of achieving exactly the effect you want. Whether you use bold, striking colour effects or subtle, pastel shades, bear in mind that the colours you choose for the frame should help to enrich those used in the picture.

For the best results, choose from colours that are used in the picture. For example, a bright red frame for a soft pastel print is unlikely to work, yet it may make a black and white photograph look striking.

Painting a mirror frame is particularly easy because the design can be as bold and bright as you like. If the mirror is a large one, and an important feature of a room, then choose colours that fit in with the way the room is decorated.

Choosing a picture

Select some printed matter that you particularly like, such as a postcard, a favourite greetings card, or a family photograph. This can be used as the inspiration for the decoration of the frame.

Selecting a frame

It does not matter if the frames are shabby or chipped because you can renovate them. You need to fill cracks and rub down the surface of all frames before painting them.

Plain, wooden frames are ideal for decorating because their porous texture absorbs paint easily. Hunt for cheap, wooden frames, or old discarded frames, as your imagination will transform them into something fresh and new. Metal, plastic and other materials also work well if the correct paints are used. Avoid ornate frames, which are fiddly to paint because the result can look overdone.

▷ *The striking colours used to decorate this Impressionist-style frame were taken from the violets and blues in the print itself. The frame was painted with a background colour, then dotted with a different colour.*

Materials and equipment

Home decorators will already have some basic materials, such as filler and sandpaper which are needed to repair old frames. But, for a really decorative finish, visit your local art shop for a wider range of brightly coloured paints.

Filler

Before priming the frame, fill all cracks and chips with a very fine decorator's filler. Many frames, even new ones, have small gaps where the mitred corners meet. These should be filled and sanded so that the surface is even.

Primer

Once the surface of the wooden frames has been prepared, they must also be primed before being painted. Acrylic gesso is an ideal base because it gives a smooth, white finish.

Alternatively, you can apply two coats of white household emulsion to the frame before adding colours. However, since household primers and undercoats are both oily, they should not be used under water-based emulsion or acrylic paints.

Paints

Acrylic paints are the most suitable paints for this type of decorative work, because they are hardwearing and can be used on wood, metal, plaster and plastic. Available from most art shops, acrylics are water-based, quick-drying and come in a wide range of colours.

Household emulsion paint can be used on most frames but it is less durable than acrylic paint. It may get scratched or chipped when used on smooth surfaces, such as plastic but it works well on wood.
Enamel paints can be used on metal, plastic and lacquered frames. They are available from craft or art shops. The drying times of different makes vary considerably, and many enamels have to be diluted with a proprietary solvent.

Varnish

Leave the frames to dry thoroughly once they have been painted. When dry, most painted frames should be sealed and finished with at least two coats of protective varnish. To seal acrylic and emulsion paints use either an acrylic varnish or a special acrylic medium, available from art shops. One exception is enamel paint, which has a hard, non-porous surface, and therefore does not need to be varnished.

Brushes

Depending on the design and the size of your frame, you will need a selection of brushes. A small water-colour brush is essential for painting any fine details on the frames. One or two larger brushes are useful for painting broader areas of colour. Use a small decorating brush for applying primer and varnish. Clean all brushes immediately after use.

Painting a wooden frame

Wooden frames are the easiest to use for a first project. Choose a picture that can be brought to life with a simple repeat pattern on the frame. Prime and seal the frame, and you are ready to paint.

You will need

◇ Acrylic paint in various colours
◇ Acrylic gesso
◇ Acrylic medium or acrylic varnish
◇ Selection of sable or hair artists' brushes
◇ Small decorator's brush
◇ Fine sandpaper
◇ Interior Polyfilla
◇ Palette or dishes for mixing paint

1 Fill any cracks or chips in the frame with fine decorator's filler. When the filler is dry, thoroughly rub down the frame with fine sandpaper.

2 Apply at least two coats of acrylic gesso or other primer, allowing each coat to dry before applying the next. If necessary, give the frame a rub down with sandpaper between coats.

3 Use a sharp pencil to draw the design on to the primed frame. Apply the paint one colour at a time, allowing each colour to dry before attempting to paint an adjoining colour.

4 Finally, when the paint is dry, apply at least two coats of varnish to protect the paint.

If the frame is flat, you can include the mitred corners into your design.

Alternatively, ignore the diagonal mitred lines and take your design to the edge of the frame.

When painting a moulded frame, the mitres cannot be ignored. The design you choose must follow the contours and ridges of the moulding and take into account the shape of the corners.

◁ *For a different look, try immitating Indian black lacquer. Paint the frame and mount black and draw the lines on with a gold felt-tip paint pen. Fill in the flowers on the mount with deep blue acrylic paint.*

INDEX

A

Acetate stencils, 68, 70
Acrylic gesso, 93
Acrylic paint
  bambooing, 58
  block printing, 84
  colourwashing, 16
  dragging, 24
  painting frames, 93
  painting on furniture, 88
  spattering, 19
  spray stencilling, 78
  stencilling, 68
Acrylic varnish stains, 45
Aerosol paints, spray stencilling, 77-82
Ageing and antique effects
  cissing, 63
  crackle varnish, 34
  dry scumbling, 52
Artist's oil colours
  bambooing, 58
  combing, 40
  crackle varnish effect, 34
  marbling, 55
  porphyry, 65
  spattering, 19
  stippling, 29
  tortoiseshelling, 62

B

Bambooing, 57-60
Bathrooms, rag rolling, 10
Beeswax polish, 33
Blanket boxes, dragging, 25
Bleaching wood, 45
Block printing, 83-6
Borders
  spray stencilling, 78-82
  stencilling, 71-6
Brushes
  bambooing, 58
  colourwashing, 16
  dragging, 24
  marbling, 55
  painting frames, 94
  painting on furniture, 88
  spattering, 20-1
  staining wood, 45
  stencilling, 68
  stippling, 28-9
  tortoiseshelling, 62

C

Ceramic paints, painting on furniture, 88, 90
Ceramics, spattering, 22
Cissing, 63
Cleaning brushes, 55, 68
Cloths

porphyry, 66
staining wood, 45
tortoiseshelling, 62, 63
Colour shading, stencilling, 69
Colours
  colourwashing, 15, 16
  combing, 41
  crackleglaze, 33
  dragging, 26
  dry scumbling, 50
  marbling, 54-5
  painting frames, 92
  painting on furniture, 89
  porphyry, 65
  ragging, 7, 9
  sponging, 12, 14
  spray stencilling, 78
  stippling, 28, 29, 30
  tortoiseshelling, 62, 64
  watercolour washes, 36
Colourwashing, 15-18
Combing, 39-42
Corners
  painting frames, 94
  stencilling borders, 72
Cotton, ragging, 9
Crackleglaze, 31-4
Craft paints, spattering, 20
Crayons, stencilling, 68
Crazing, crackleglaze, 31-4

D

Decorator's brushes
  bambooing, 58
  colourwashing, 17
  dragging, 24
  painting frames, 94
  painting on furniture, 88
  spattering, 20, 21
Designs
  enlarging, 89
  transferring, 88
Distressing, 52
Doors
  painting on, 90
  staining, 44
Dragging, 23-6
Dry scumbling, 49-52

E

Eggshell paint
  bambooing, 58
  colourwashing, 16
  combing, 40
  dragging, 24
  marbling, 54
  sponging, 13
  stencilling, 68
  stippling, 29
Emulsion paint
  block printing, 84
  colourwashing, 15, 16
  combing, 40
  crackleglaze, 32, 33

dragging, 24
painting frames, 93
painting on furniture, 88
spattering, 19
sponging, 12, 13
stencilling, 68
watercolour washes, 36
Enamel paints
  painting frames, 93
  spattering, 20
Enlarging designs, 89

F

Fabric paints, spattering, 20
Fabrics
  block printing, 84
  spray stencilling, 78, 79-80
Fans, combing, 41
Fantasy effects
  bambooing, 57-60
  porphyry, 65-6
  tortoiseshelling, 61-4
Feathers, marbling, 55
Filler, 93
Fitches, 62, 63, 66
Floggers, 16, 17, 24
Floors
  staining, 43, 44, 45
  marbling, 54
Frames, painting, 91-4
Furniture
  combing, 39, 40
  distressing, 52
  dry scumbling, 50, 51
  painting on, 87-90
  staining, 43, 44
  watercolour washes, 36-8

G

Gesso, 93
Gilding, ageing, 52
Glasspaper, 88
Glazes
  bambooing, 58
  colourwashing, 15
  combing, 40
  dragging, 24
  marbling, 54
  ragging, 9
  scumbling, 48
  sponging, 12-13
  stippling, 29
  tortoiseshelling, 62
Gloss paint
  combing, 40
  marbling, 54
Gouache, watercolour washes, 36
Graining see Combing; Dragging
Gum arabic, crackleglaze, 32, 33

H

Hair combs, 40

I

Inks, watercolour washes, 36

K

Knotting, 45

L

Lacquer, imitation, 94

M

Manila card stencils, 68, 70
Marbling, 53-6
  spattering, 20-1
  spray stencilling, 78
Metal paints, painting on
  furniture, 88
Mirror frames, painting, 92
Mitring corners, stencil borders,
  72
Motifs, stencilling borders, 72

O

Oil-based paints
  combing, 40
  crackle varnish effect, 34
  crackleglaze, 32
  dragging, 24
  marbling, 54-5
  scumbling, 48
  spattering, 19
  sponging, 12
  stencilling, 68
  tortoiseshelling, 62
Oil glaze see Transparent oil glaze
Over-grainers, 16

P

Patterns
  colourwashing, 17
  combing, 42
Pictures, painting frames, 91-4
Pine furniture, staining, 44
Plaster of Paris, 58
Polyurethane varnish
  bambooing, 58
  crackleglaze, 33
  stains, 45
  stencilling, 68
  tortoiseshelling, 62
Porphyry, 65-6
Potato printing, 84
Primer, 93
Printing, block, 83-6
PVA paint, block printing, 84

R

Rag rolling, 7-10
Ragging, 7-9
Rags
  dragging, 25
  marbling, 55
Rollers
  block printing, 84
  stippling, 29
Rolling, rag, 7-10

S

Safety, ragging, 9
Sanding, 45, 63
Screens, watercolour washes, 37-8
Scrumbling, 47-8
Scumble glaze see Transparent oil
  glaze
Scumbling, 47-8
  dry scumbling, 49-52
Shading, stencilling, 69
Skirtings, staining, 44
Spattering, 19-22
  porphyry, 65
Spatulas, combing, 40
Sponges
  block printing, 84, 85-6
  marbling, 55
  sponging, 11-14
  stencilling, 68
  stippling, 29
Spray stencilling, 77-82
Staining wood, 43-6
Stencilling, 67-70
  borders, 71-6
  spattering, 20, 21-2
  spray stencilling, 77-82
Stippling, 27-30
Stippling brushes, 28-9
Stripes
  colourwashing, 18
  rag rolling, 10

T

Templates, painting on furniture,
  89
  see also Stencilling
Texture, colourwashing, 17
Tortoiseshelling, 61-4
Tracing stencils, 73
Transferring designs, 88
Transparent oil glaze
  bambooing, 58

colourwashing, 15
combing, 40
dragging, 24
marbling, 54
ragging, 9
scumbling, 48
sponging, 12-13
stippling, 29
tortoiseshelling, 62
Trays, sponging, 12-13

U

Universal stainers, 12, 55, 58

V

Varnish
  bambooing, 58
  combing, 40
  crackle varnish effect, 34
  crackleglaze, 32, 33
  dry scumbling, 51
  painting frames, 93
  painting on furniture, 88
  staining wood, 45
  stencilling, 68
  tortoiseshelling, 62
  watercolour washes, 36

W

Walls
  colourwashing, 15
  combing, 41
  dry scumbling, 50, 51
  rag rolling, 7-10
  ragging, 7-9
  sponging, 13
Watercolour washes, 35-8
Wax polish, 33
White spirit
  cleaning brushes, 55
  combing, 40
  marbling, 55
  safety, 9
  stippling, 29
  tortoiseshelling, 62
Wood-graining see Combing;
  Dragging
Wood-graining combs, 40
Woodwork
  combing, 41
  painting frames, 92, 94
  staining, 43-6
  stencilling, 67

PHOTOGRAPHIC CREDITS
Front Cover IPC Magazines/Robert Harding Syndication, 1 EWA/Di Lewis, 2-3 Heritage Bathrooms ltd, 4-5 IPC Magazines/Robert Harding Syndication, 6 Elrose Products ltd, 7 Crown Paints, 8 EWA, 9(l) Crown Paints, 9(r) Mal Stone/Eaglemoss, 10 Crown Paints, 11 Living Magazine, 12-14 John Suett/Eaglemoss, 15 EWA/ Spike POwell, 16-17, 18(t) Ian Howes/Eaglemoss, 18(l) EWA/Andrea Von Einseidel, 18(r) Collins and Brown, 19 Steve Tanner/Eaglemoss, 20-22 Ian Howes/Eaglemoss, 25(b) Collins and Brown, 27-29 John Suett/Eaglemoss, 31 Steve Tanner/Eaglemoss, 35-38, 39, 41 100 Idees, 40 Martin Norris/Eaglemoss, 43 Modes et Travaux, 44, 45(l) IPC Magazines, 47,48 Shona Wood/Eaglemoss, 49-52(t) Steve Tanner/Eaglemoss, 52(b) Bridgeman Art Library, 53 Fritz Von Der Schulenberg, 54 Steve Tanner/Eaglemoss,55-56 Modes et travaux, 57 Royal Pavillion, Brighton, 58

Garden Picture Library, 60(l) Martin Norris/Eaglemoss, 60(r) Toucan Books, 61 Freda Parker/Eaglemoss, 62 Bridgeman Art Library, 64(l) EWA/Frank Herholdt, 64(r) Simon Butcher/Eaglemoss, 65, 66 Zed Nelson/Eaglemoss, 67 Steve Tanner/Eaglemoss, 68(t) EWA/David Cripps, 68(b) Steve Tanner/Eaglemoss, 69 100 Idees, 70 Felicity Benyon Stencil Kits, 71 IPC Magazines/Robert Harding Syndication, 73 Steve Tanner/Eaglemoss, 76 Jon Bouchier, 77,78 John Suett/Eaglemoss, 83,84 100 Idees, 85 Crown Paints, 86 Collins and Brown, 87,88,89 Crown Paints, 90(t,br) 100 Idees, 90(bl) Houses and Interiors, 91,92,93 Steve Tanner/Eaglemoss, 94 Salamander Books.

Key: EWA = Elizabeth Whiting and Associates